AF391913

Tales of
Young Patriots

P. Norman Grant

La Maison Publishing
Vero Beach, Florida
The Hibiscus City
lamaisonpublishing@gmail.com

*To the students of my past,
who taught me how to teach.*

Introduction

Tales of Young Patriots is a collection of twelve exciting short stories for middle or high school social studies students. Whether in a classroom or just casual reading at home, these snapshots of American history help explain how our country was created with the help of young adults.

From the ocean passages of the 1600s to our modern desert wars, Young Patriots contains lessons of virtue driven by action. Great for additions to an academic setting, vacation reading, or actual test material with questions and answers included, Tales of Young Patriots will stir the imagination of young adults.

From the author

I hope these stories give students a fuller picture of some of our American past. As a Viet Nam veteran who then went off to Woodstock and the University of California Berkeley, I got to live through a lot of history. As young adults read more in their civics, history, or social studies classes, may the sights and sounds of a country come alive. Encourage class discussions with the big ideas and discover how they relate to our time. And for all our future patriots, don't forget to make some history of your own.

--P. Norman Grant

Table of Contents

Part One

Part I includes another view of the Salem witch trials explaining a mysterious phenomenon. During the War of 1812, a young man dodges the British warships while the Star Spangled Banner is being written, and two boys of different races team up to survive a Civil War battle.

Judgement at Sea

Sailing the Atlantic Ocean

Billy lost track of how many days they had been to sea. He had to check his primitive calendar carved on the side of his black leather boots. Down near the heel, he would slice a notch for every sunset he saw from the ship. Billy cut notches when he couldn't see the sun because of a rainstorm, but he knew well enough when nighttime had come.

Why did his parents have to leave their native land? He still couldn't figure it out. At 15 years of age, there was a lot he couldn't comprehend. Why did his father close the butcher shop in London? He remembered something about the high cost of operating the business. And something about belonging to the wrong church. His father's customers were told to go down the street to another shop to buy their meats because his competitor went to the right church.

He did know that the Church of England was becoming more oppressive, and it wouldn't be long before its officers threw the non-believers into dungeons. People lost their social status, businesses, and even lives because of this intolerance. Even if you were a Roman Catholic or Puritan, or another Protestant, your family might feel the consequences of not being in the favored majority.

Now he was at sea, a thousand miles from anywhere, and England would be a land of remembrances, maybe forever. Billy stared into the dark waters and thought of what would come in the colonies. They were going to a place called Virginia, but very few ships had returned from there with men who could describe it.

Billy saw a group of sailors sitting around a barrel on the foredeck playing cards. This journey is such a gamble, he thought. It's much more of a risk than what those men were gambling. They would bring a sea bag, the shoes they wore, and maybe a book or two if they could read. His parents brought everything they owned. The oaken chest of drawers, the rocker, the knife collection his father planned to use in the colonies, and of course, the family Bible. And every stitch of clothing they had in the world was stuffed inside the large, brass-bound trunk.

With his parents, Mr. and Mrs. Wilson, tucked into the bed rolls below decks, Billy began wandering around the top deck. It was a calm, warm June evening with a new moon lingering above the clouds. A few people were up top, taking in the fresh air. As he looked above, he could see that the sails were not being pushed out and forward with enough strength to gather enough speed for the boat.

"Pardon me, sir," Billy asked a sailor standing with his pipe against a railing. "How many days away are we?"

A smile slowly grew across his bearded face but stopped before it became a joyful expression. It was more like a painful smile. "Laddy, even the best captains cannot predict within a week when we get to the New World. With wind like this, it could take 'til Christmas.'

The boy looked out over the gently rolling swells and wondered how it would be to sail out on these oceans most of the days of your life, like this bearded sailor in front of him. Billy asked, "But it's better for you than that gale we had last week. That was like the whole world turned upside down."

"Naw, that wasn't hardly nothin' Laddy. Now, if you ever round Cape Horn from the West, now you've got yourself a real blow. Say, aren't you the butcher's boy?"

Guessing that the crew knew much about the passengers it was taking across the ocean, he said, "True enough."

"Well then, we might have need of his services to prepare a couple of those sheep below. The dried meat is running low, and there's no hint of land. Well, have a good night, Laddy." With that, the sailor turned his boots around and headed toward the card game on the foredeck.

Billy thought it couldn't get any rougher in that gale. Where in the world was Cape Horn? All he knew was that it had been 26 days and nights, and it was not a very placid crossing until now. He was finding out that calm winds are not the best to have either. Was their vessel just a speck in the hands of fate? Mother Nature ruled passengers and crew more than the captain did.

The ship's name was carved in massive gold painted letters into the stern, and it described the 200 passengers and crew as Courageous. Beneath that in smaller letters: London. All aboard were indeed brave to take on this adventure, and all 200 were sure of very little.

Some were regretful. During the violent storm last week, Mr. and Mrs. Whiteside's precious daughter fell overboard in the middle of the night within view of Mr. Smithers, the watch captain. She was only nine years old and wanted to see the lightning. Now the Whitesides' wished they never left Brighton and would like nothing better than to be back in view of the cliffs of Dover. But they were moving on.

More than the weather was on Billy's mind. Supplies were getting low. Fresh water and fresh vegetables were always a problem on long ocean voyages. He had heard men talking in his father's shop about how exact the provisioning had to be. Too many supplies would take up room for passengers and slow the ship down. Not enough food, and the captain had unhappy and unhealthy people all crammed together on a 150-foot floating community.

Scurvy was the most common affliction at sea. Men would not get enough juice, their skin would start to dry up, and their body robbed of energy. Without citrus fruits or onions for a month, a man could slowly descend into a whirlpool of pain. His gums would bleed, his lips would split open, and his skin would turn the texture of parchment. He could be found dead one morning.

So lemons from Italy, limes from Spain, and oranges from Portugal would be loaded into big wooden barrels and lowered into the hold of the Courageous. Along with jarred and dried foods were live cattle, chickens, sheep, and pigs. Some would serve fresh meat on the ship, and others would make it to their destination to flourish just as the people would. It was crucial that enough food for the trip was stored below.

The man in charge of the ship's stores would have to be precise in his buying. While on board, he would be the only man besides the captain to carry a pistol. If a man wanted an extra portion of dinner, he would have to go through the chandler, the commander of the ship's stores. The odds were not good that anyone would be given extra food. That meant passengers and crew.

The livestock were kept below. Only with smooth enough seas were the hatches on the side of the boat opened and sunlight allowed to enter. It was not a pleasant trip for the animals or those living near them. Their sounds in a windy storm would keep anyone awake, and their natural smells would sink into the fabric of every piece of clothing people near them had on.

At night, Billy sometimes found it hard to sleep when the ship rolled back and forth. For some not used to being on a sea-going vessel, this rolling would make them physically ill, and they would have to go on deck to relieve themselves. Those who became seasick would long for the sight of land most earnestly.

During these sleepless times, he would get up and go forward where the staircase was to the second level of the boat. He and his parents were booked in steerage, meaning they were staying at the very bottom of the ship where the aroma of the provisions and the live animals tied to the sides of the interior hull would remind them of their position in life.

One night he climbed the stairs to the second level and quietly sat looking at the stars through the open hatch. He couldn't go up top after dark. Since the child was washed overboard, no one except the crew would be on deck after sunset. But very near to him was an unusual noise. It sounded like an eating noise. Someone was slurping something wet. The muffled munching was so inviting he was just about to announce himself to the mystery man.

This shadow was about 20 feet away, but in the dark, he couldn't quite perceive who it was. Then he suddenly realized this was not a situation to be found in. The barrel next to the shadow had letters scrawled in a foreign language. It was the orange barrel, the most treasured stock on board. Simpson, the chandler, would not want to find anyone near it. In fact, the lid was usually sealed after the morning's dispensing of one piece of fruit per passenger.

Billy slipped back silently into a shadow and became as quiet as a cat stalking a mouse. But this was a man. Billy wondered what would happen if this figure he spied on turned and saw him, a busy body boy, witnessing such a theft. This handful of oranges in town was not worth much. But on a ship sailing the high seas, there was a different law — the law of the captain. A man could be whipped for such an act.

Billy could sniff the orange, and his nose seemed pleased with the smell. How nice it would be if he could tear open the beautiful skin and help himself to the tasty flesh of the fruit. Maybe the two of them could conspire to share the forbidden food. Should he take the chance?

The man reached up without moving from his seated position and tried to dig down into the barrel. But the level of fruit was nearing the bottom, and he would have to stand to get at them. As the shadow carefully rose, Billy could make out the facial features of Pastor Jones, the soon-to-be leader of the church in their new homeland. He looked around intently to see if anyone was watching.

The boy's heart began to pump like repeating cannons as the reverend turned his way in the dark. The light from the open hatch shined down on this man, allowing Billy to see Jones' swollen lips, sunken eyes, and thin frame. He faced the barrel and again made a dive with his desperate hands together, grabbing the remedy to his ills. The boy retreated down the stairs as the reverend, one hand bracing on the floor and one clutching the orange, sat down again.

Should he tell anyone? It would surely raise a nasty commotion for the inhabitants of this ocean-going town if he were to tell his father. He couldn't possibly inform the captain. A tale like this would ruin a man in a way, even worse than the deadly scurvy.

The act was repeated for the next two nights, and Billy became anxious about withholding the story. He would see the reverend on deck, and there was no hint of recognition of Billy's being a witness. But the boy saw that the reverend's color was returning to him. The fruit was having a beneficial effect. However, it should have been shared by everyone. Not just those who thought themselves afflicted, Billy thought.

After three days, a morning dawned under clear skies and a fair breeze. Billy awoke to a strange sound. A whistle piped up. Then a shout was heard.

"All hands and passengers up top! First mate, summon those below."

The captain had never said a word publicly on this journey, so this was a significant gesture. A mumbling could be heard as those from the three decks below shook the sleep from their heads. The sky was a glistening blue, and the ocean seemed just the slightest bit lighter in color. There was hope that this was good news.

"Shipmates and Pilgrims," he shouted from his position atop the aft deck. Everyone stood erect and at attention. "Last night, our humble ship was bumped by the welcome presence of tree stumps. Now I need not tell you what that means, but to erase any doubt, we are probably no more than a day away from shore. Exactly where that shore lies, we cannot know until we assess our surroundings. But by my calculations, we should not be far from the colony of Jamestown."

The assembled throng let go a huge cheer. Billy Wilson looked around at the smiles of the tired and hungry travelers, and as he did, he caught the eye of Pastor Jones, who gave the boy a knowing look.

The captain continued, "So be advised that we should organize our areas and be prepared to leave the vessel just as we boarded. Nothing further. God be with you all."

Just at that moment, Billy noticed something that had just fallen from the reverend's black coat. A couple of tiny orange peels had dropped unnoticed behind the man of the cloth. They were called up to the deck so early he probably didn't have a chance to throw the peels overboard.

In a smooth and efficient movement, the boy slid sideways over to the man, who was now shaking another passenger's hand. He reached down, grabbed the offending evidence, and whisked them over the side.

As the boy turned back to his mother and father, still hugging each other in the early morning light, the pastor grabbed him by the shoulder. Billy could see the tears welling up in the man's eyes. His face was a picture of suffering, and his stooped shoulders spoke of his pain. But a flicker of a smile crossed his burned and weathered lips. "Thank you," he said, grabbing Billy's hand as if the pastor had just built a brand new church in the new world.

Many challenges would test these people, Billy thought. Even a man of God is tested. He and Pastor Jones would face enough hardship once they got off the Courageous. It's best that the long and brutal voyage be forgotten. After all, it was 1642, and a whole new life awaited them.

Questions

1. How did Billy keep track of time?
    A. His watch
    B. He carved notches in his boots
    C. Marked off his calendar
    D. Remembered the number of days from land

2. The best meaning for the word "Placid" is?
    A. Disturbing
    B. Stormy
    C. Peaceful
    D. Dangerous

3. Why was the name Courageous an appropriate name?
    A. The pilgrims were courageous.
    B. It was a long journey
    C. They would be fortunate to survive
    D. They were all poor people

4. What was a major problem on the ship?
    A. Theft
    B. Fighting
    C. Scurvy
    D. Seasickness

5. Where were the lemons, limes, and oranges from?
    A. France, England, and Italy
    B. Italy, Spain, and Portugal
    C. Spain
    D. Italy and Spain

6. Why did people get Scurvy?
    A. Not eating enough
    B. Not enough water
    C. Not eating the right foods
    D. Because they were seasick

In a paragraph, what kind of secret would you be willing to keep and why?

Witch Hunt

Magical or Mythical

The winter of 1692 was a cold one in New England. If a man didn't have a daily job, he would be chopping enough firewood to keep the house that he lived in warm. Those who farmed couldn't tend their fields through the mounds of windblown snow. Their livestock would stay in the barns, not leaving the stalls, and not fed well because of the difficulty of moving so much grain around through such freezing conditions. Cows, pigs, and all kinds of fowl would spend months inside, never seeing the sky. Many would die.

Young Elizabeth and Mary also had to remain indoors for long periods. The two girls were to read the Bible and learn to knit just as their mothers would. But often, this was not amusement enough for two girls just entering their womanly years.

"Elizabeth, did you see the way young William Cory spied me at the Meeting today?" Mary asked, wanting to get her mind away from the gray wool threads on her lap. "He had that look in his eye as if he were interested in talking to me. How can I be released from Mother for a moment next Sunday to see what his talk would be of?"

"Mary, one is supposed to be interested only in the Holy Scripture at Meeting. Not in finding young boys to talk to," Elizabeth said, frowning. Then, quickly with a playful grin, "But I would be glad to distract your mother for a few minutes. Perhaps I could ask her opinion of Reverend Parris' sermon, and she would be glad to give it."

Mary welcomed Elizabeth's hand in the conspiracy. Anything would serve to spice up a life of drudgery, cold, and containment in a town where if one were to laugh, a score of tense people would sneer and wonder why. "And did you see Mrs. Corey turn to gape at us? His mother looks as if she thinks she is 'Holier than Thou' and with very little reason. Fortunately, William seems nothing like his prune of a parent!" Elizabeth turned to leave for her father's horse and wagon, then back to her friend. She lowered her voice and said, "I'll be by this afternoon for the 'other meeting' if all goes well." One eyebrow slowly rose.

Because the sky was gray and the snow seemed as if it would just keep piling up until March, the villagers of Salem walked around with the usual solemn expressions, dressed in dreary dark cloaks. And the message from the pulpit that

Sunday was not very cheerful either. It aroused little hope in their heavy lives to hear Pastor Parris say they were all sinners, salvation from a fiery hell, a faint glimmer on the New England horizon.

It was predestination, he said, that bound the people forever to sin. Their destiny was to be a sinner forever, and only by admitting to their sinfulness could they be saved by the Almighty on Judgement Day. That day seemed too far away, especially for two young girls of the Massachusetts Bay Colony.

Later that afternoon, a group of girls found their way to Mary Putnam's house, the biggest home in town. Mr. Putnam served as the town's judge, so not surprisingly, he could afford a servant.

"Tituba, tell me who my husband will be," Mary demanded. "Is he now in Salem Village?" Six girls sat in a semi-circle around the dark Caribbean woman, keeping their voices low even though the Putnam's weren't expected back to the house soon. They would not look kindly on the future-telling powers of a slave being passed on to their daughter and her friends.

But so eager were the girls for news of the future that they brought gifts to Tituba of candy and colored yarn. They begged her with their eyes to reveal the mysteries that might only be solved with magic. In Salem, women and girls worked with their hands at the spinning wheels to make cloth, grinding grains to make flour, and reading the Bible at night by a low candlelight. The only real social gathering through the winter remained the Sunday Meeting at the Church.

The young girls had other ideas about the strict social codes of their parents and the Church. If the pastor was already calling them sinners, why not enjoy the sin and have the island woman tell their future? Tituba leaned back in a shabby work dress, closed her eyes, and ran her fingers over a small doll.

"I see a boy in a high tree. He has yellow hair, and he calls for someone." She rocked back and forth and then swayed from side to side as she sat on the floor of the darkened kitchen. Soon, she would be cooking dinner at the hearth for the Putnams, but for now, she moaned mysteriously, captivating the girls who looked on in awe.

"Yellow hair. That must be Miles. I knew it! He calls for me." Mary could hardly contain her amazement. "I remember seeing him in a tree near the square just after sundown." Thin little Mary began to rock herself side to side with her legs crossed on the cold cabin floor, mimicking Tituba's rhythm.

"Oh please, Tituba, you must find my love," Mary begged.

Elizabeth, with her long red hair, slid forward on the floor to press the woman into action for her, too. Tituba slowly opened her eyes and gazed slowly from one face to another in the group. Her soul seemed to be on the outside of the gathering, looking in.

Tituba hummed in a low pitch, "Me-oh. Who is da man?" She slowly opened her eyes, but the object of her sight was far away. Maybe it was in another world. "Who's the man in black, and why he no like the girl? Why she afraid, oh Me-oh?" She rocked herself heavily, then formed a big question mark with her eye brows. "Who is the big man in black?"

While the girls looked on, knees trembled, legs twitched, and lips quivered in anticipation. Tituba rubbed a raggedy doll and drew a circle in the ashes she had scooped from the hearth. After a few silent minutes, she x-ed the circle out. And with determination, mumbled, "No more!"

"No more. The spirit is tired. The veil cannot be lifted. You go home now," Tituba said as she opened her eyes. She squinted, a little frightened and exhausted at the same time.

The young girls seemed to come out of a trance.

"Oh!" Mary cried and looked over the group of girls around her. "I was away from here. Where were we?"

Tituba looked up and slowly raised her big body to stare straight ahead.

"WHO GOES THERE?" Mr. Putnam stood six-feet tall in the doorway of the darkened home. He was not expected back this soon, but here he was, gazing at the strange assemblage in HIS kitchen. "Tituba, dismiss these children. Get that fire going and fix us some supper!" He crossed his arms imperiously. "What are you all waiting for? GO HOME!"

Mary winced in embarrassment. Little Elizabeth started to tremble. The huge man wore a large dark cape and blasted his voice with thunderous force into the kitchen. On unsteady legs, the girls jumped up, looking sheepishly at each other. Mary wondered, What did Mr. Putnam see? This was not a Godly gathering. Reverend Parris would not approve.

*****

In the days that followed, words filled the town with the gossip of Tituba and her magic. Or was it witchcraft? Strange stories of unusual behavior began seeping into every home. Goody Carrier was seen talking with dogs who spoke back to her. Annie Osborne said she saw Tituba riding a broomstick in the sky, and a staid and suspicious Mr. Burroughs crossed the street rather than get near the Putnam home. There could be a witch in the judge's own home. The townspeople traded stories they heard or even imagined they heard. The fear of witchcraft sailed across the ocean as new arrivals from Britain brought more dark tails of the devil's work to the new Colony. Yet those accused in the New World always seemed to have a personal rival pointing a finger at them. Were these feelings of mystery or plain animosity?

"That woman puts her hair up too high and exalts herself o'er much when she walks down the street," one portly wife would loudly report from an evening's sewing circle.

"Witch!" her friends would cry. "She travels with Satan when the sun goes down."

"I saw Bridget Wallcott holding hands with that boy William Cory, then they slid along a tree branch together," another girl whispered to a gaggle of friends on a street corner. "Witch!" they mumbled as one. Then, while the accusations flew, they pointed at poor Sarah Frye with her disheveled frock and her downcast countenance, ambling slowly in the chilly afternoon air. Suddenly, Sarah looked over nervously at the girls.

"Wouldn't surprise me if she's a sister of that island gal, Tituba. Looks like a witch to me," another mean-spirited voice would wail. The young girls followed their own misgivings as stories grew like weeds. But when word got back to Rev. Parris, the only clergy in town, he thought of an idea for a sermon that might lessen the tension.

That Sunday, the Reverend asked for a full house to assemble. He promised to expose the work of the devil that day, so the whole town was buzzing. On a warming April morning, there sat the six girls who had met with Tituba and heard her spectral visions. While the full congregation entered full of curiosity, the row of girls began to giggle uncontrollably.

As Reverend Parris began the service, each one of them started to twitch. Arms flailed, legs jumped, heads shook. Just when sad Sarah Frye arrived late, as usual, frayed coat drawn tightly around herself, young Abigail Goode started to moan. The rest of the girls all turned around at once and spied the poor old woman. All six of them began to close their eyes at the same time and emitted a series of little shrieks as if they were spotting mice. "EEK, EEK, EEK," they cackled.

Reverend Parris stopped the service and looked down at the commotion. With a sigh, he began again the sermon of "fire and brimstone" that was to greet each sinner eventually. Then, one of the girls sneezed. Suddenly, the whole row of girls began to sneeze with her. Sarah Frye lurched forward to glare at them. The six girls turned around as one to the whole congregation and imitated Sarah's disapproval by sticking out their tongues.

One church member whispered to another, "It's as if they are in concert. Every movement was performed as if they were on a stage and not in a Puritan church service."

Suddenly, Mary looked up and began to follow something flying above her. "There she is now with the yellow bird. She has the bird sucking at her finger, where the witch spot is. Sarah Frye does not sit here but flies to the top of this room! And she pinches me when she flies low to do so."

Mary had half-closed her eyes as she droned out her scenario. And at one moment, the other girls erupted with "Ow! And she pinches me."

"I've been stabbed!"

"She bites me!"

The congregation was stunned. The Reverend looked dumbfounded. Nearby, Mr. Putnam along with the church elders standing throughout the building, looked on with suspicious silence. The congregation recoiled in horror.

"You are a witch lady!" cried the six girls in unison, turning to face poor Sarah Frye. With one practiced voice, they snarled their bile.

All those present had believed in witches because to believe in God is to believe in God's adversary. The devil was never far from the Reverend's sermons. Even Cotton Mather, that great speaker and writer from Boston, would impress the citizenry of the Bay Colony with cases of witchcraft. Cattle would die for no apparent reason; Mather blamed it on witches. Friendly Indians would start a warpath chant; it was the work of wizards. Disease would spread unchecked throughout New England; this was the fury of Satan in the form of witches, the devil, and his servants. And the people in Salem were hungry to find the witches.

The uproar of the congregation was such that Reverend Parris had to stop the service. He immediately stepped down and walked over to Judge Putnam. After conferring, they began to clear the room that was still buzzing with the talk of Sarah being accused so venomously. The six girls were invited to stay, and the accused was told to wait inside the foyer, next to the huge oaken door. The simple, log building with the high ceiling, which had just been a church, would now be a courthouse.

Outside the church doors, the town folk were chattering.

"Isn't that the Sarah Frye who dresses in rags, does no work, and begs for food?"

"The same," one woman said.

"And isn't Sarah the one who goes against you in the courts in the inheritance matter?" one man asked with a sneer.

"The same."

"And isn't Tituba that servant who would defile our Puritan religion by bringing her own God from the islands?" The crowd was becoming more indignant.

"The same. If we let these evil doers live carefree in Salem, we will all be afflicted, in one manner or another, my dear friend."

Mary's mother appeared and whispered to Mrs. Putnam, who stood with the others.

"My daughter has told me herself that she has seen Goody Carrier talking to the dogs, and they talking back to her. The midwife that she is should not be trusted to deliver newborns to this Christian land. Only a man from a Puritan school like Harvard should be bringing new life to Salem, not a witch! We should discuss this with Reverend Parris." Each tale piled on top of others.

Parris had seen such in England, where they burned witches at the stake by the score. In France and in Spain, women under suspicion would be hanged for questionable offenses. In Salem, if you denied you were a witch, THAT was proof enough that you were guilty. However, who was afflicting whom? Behind every accusation, there seemed to be other reasons for the charge. Long-standing feuds would end up in witch trials. If a farmer's pigs were to graze across his neighbor's property, one would tell of the other's wife suspiciously walking late at night in the woods. Rivals in love would accuse each other. Anyone could be locked up indefinitely.

This day was different. With a burst of the Meeting Hall doors, Reverend Parris emerged closely followed by Judge Putnam rushed forward with a furor. "My towns folk, we have been deceived. Our young girls have sinned in our company and confessed to having sport with us. Sarah Frye may go as free as anyone here, but Mary and Elizabeth have something to say."

From behind the huge caped figure of Putnam crept two frightened children soaking in guilt. Elizabeth could not speak at all. Mary, weeping, stepped forward. Rev. Parris stood by with a painful smile.

"We beg forgiveness, Mother, Father, Judge Putnam. We accuse no one. Childish play may be as sinful as the evil that men do. We see no witches, but I feel we had a taste of the Devil in us when we played. My only wish is for others to see the spectral visions as the result of imagination. Other images may only be the failings of human nature. Colored vindictiveness, jealousy, or plain prejudice covered by a mystical story." Mary bowed her head in humility.

With that, the remaining girls quietly slinked out of the building into the crowd of villagers and reached out to their anxious parents. Extra chores and memorizing more Bible verses were in store for them. Hope would be that Salem might see with clearer vision and the end to the Witch Trials of the New World.

Questions

1. What was Parris' occupation?
    A. shoemaker
    B. judge
    C pastor
    D. soldier

2. Where was Salem?
    A. England
    B. New England
    C. Massachusetts Bay colony
    D. Boston

3. Who led the group of girls?
    A. Ann
    B. Mary and Elizabeth
    C. Tituba
    S. Mercy

4. What was the punishment for being a witch?
    A. burning at the stake
    B. being hanged
    C. long jail sentence
    D. Either A. B. or C.

5. What did Mary pretend to see in the church?
    A. a ghost
    B. a trick
    C. a yellow bird
    D. a witch

6. In a paragraph, what did the villagers learn from this episode?

Surprise at Ft. Ticonderoga

Meeting with Nathan at the Gate

Emily's father said she was in a grand place in historic times. She should be happy that she came to Ft. Ticonderoga.

"Look at the beautiful ice-covered lake and the gorgeous geese and the mountains of pine all around. Back in Birmingham, we'd just stare at each other and the large ill-fragrant paper mill. You wouldn't want to be back there now, would you?" he would say.

Emily's mother and she took an oath during the coldest part of the winter that they would never complain until they were relieved of duty here on the colonial frontier. Neither would make her feelings known to Father. He was fortunate enough to be a gunnery sergeant since he might not have been promoted so quickly if he were back in England. It took a special soldier. Mr. Wolfe would tell his family to serve the King in such a primitive area of the world. But he was bound and determined to fulfill his tour of duty.

"Daughter, you'll be looking at an officer one day soon, and you'll have all the finest things that London can provide. Your mother knows this is the best place for us right now. With all the patience a brave girl like you can muster, we'll all do just fine."

Emily folded the red military jacket, carried it into her parent's bedroom, and placed it on the bed. As she looked around at the stone walls, Emily knew there was no sense in whining about her lot in life. Even though there were no other girls her age here, no games to play, and no boys to dance with here in Godforsaken, New York, somehow, she would survive and see the white cliffs of Dover, England, once again. But she must return before she's too old to be chosen as a wife. Sixteen was an advanced age to start the matrimony game, she thought.

"Father, not that we would ever want a war to come, but it seems that we won't accomplish our mission until the army gains a victory. I long to see the dresses in the storefronts and smell the fine sausages cooking on Queens St. I'm growing up inside a stone house in the middle of a wilderness."

Emily furrowed her eyebrows in a plea while her mother was in the cupboard foraging for tea. She didn't want to hear this conversation. Her father slowly took a seat in the middle of the one large room made entirely of huge stones. The floor, the walls, and the ceiling were all constructed of natural rock.

It sometimes seemed as if her father were made of the same elements.

"My darling, we are but a tiny dot in England's plan to govern this wild territory, but carry out that plan we must. Most of these colonists are law-abiding citizens loyal to the Crown. They would like nothing more than for these terrorists to take off to Canada or disappear into the great ocean. But unfortunately, it may take some time to rid ourselves of the likes of these frontiersmen who claim the King's land for their own. I would push them myself toward the depths right now if I thought it could gain peace among the people." He sat down and lit his long pipe.

Emily sniffed the smoke from rich Virginia tobacco. "Captain De la Place says now that spring is upon us, someone will make a move soon. Is that true, Father?"

"True enough, my little one. The English Army has not yet landed enough troops from her ships on Lake Champlain to fight a real military force. The cannons inside this fort should be reason enough to fear not the raggedy men of the Vermont Territory," her father said with pride.

She was getting rumors from outside Ft. Ticonderoga's walls, but God forbid he knew the source.

Emily looked out through the only window their family's home had. It was a narrow opening with a thick layer of glass through which she could barely make out the other side of the lake. But her mind's eye could survey the scene and see the Green Mountains that the French named Verdmont in the distance. The green mountains still contained a white frosting on top as the winter snow had not yet melted.

She also recalled the sound at night of ice cracking on the lake. Lying asleep, she could hear the loud snapping and twisting as the water transformed back into an inky blue from

January's icy white. The frightening noise would awaken Emily as she sat upright in the bed that jutted from the stone wall beside the fireplace. And she would think of Nathan. Could he be the one who would save her from this hellish existence?

"Emily, you have the most beautiful skin," he would say, "like the color of a New Hampshire oyster." Out of the clear blue sky, he would say these things. But these words came from the mouth of a boy who rarely bathed, wore animal skins for clothes, and made his living running errands for Emily's enemies who not allowed inside Ft. Ticonderoga. Nathan was more a servant than a man, and he was an ambitious native.

Her mother would look away when he would ask for Emily once inside the walls. After Nathan would unload his wagon of firewood, a basket of fish, or his occasional box of wildflowers, they would share their teenage hearts and talk of the hopes and dreams of the young.

"When the colonies are free, Emily, I will have my own carriage business and ride happy citizens between Boston and the countryside. You will be back in England with some fancy Count, Duke, or some such." He had the most amusing gleam to his eye when he would butter up his words. "I shall be bouncing three children on my two knees while you debate the merits of your horses and the fitness of your hunting dogs near some town that ends with 'shire,' and we'll remember when we were talking here inside the walls of Ft. Ticonderoga." His dancing blue eyes would sparkle with his teasing.

He was a Vermonter, officially the enemy, but his services were crucial. Besides trading with the Mohawks, the soldiers had very few comforts, so Nathan served as a middleman for those who lived inside the star-shaped stone fortress. He handled the goods and services of those hunters and farmers in the area and brought them to Ft. Ti.

Emily remembered Madam De la Place's giving Nathan a small pistol for a box of face powder. The wife of the outpost's commander was desperate for a touch of civilization. She complained she would rather be with her husband on a battlefield against Genghis Khan than be stuck in the middle of a million trees waiting to assist the King. Emily turned away from the window and ate a dinner of rabbit that the hunters were lucky enough to shoot that day. Her parents ate joylessly. Still thinking of Nathan and his resourcefulness, she asked, "Father, are all the Vermonters our enemy?"

"No lass, only those who would take the King's land despite the proper deeds kept by the British land agents in Albany. Those animal skin-wearing thieves are calling this land their own, and their leader, Ethan Allen, has a price on his head. He's the one who has the locals all excited. But these rows of cannons say they'll not come across that lake for any other reason than to stand trial in Loyalist Albany." Her father grew stern, picked up the roasted rabbit leg, and chewed into it as if it were the last food the forest would yield.

The next day Nathan came again. He was well-recognized at the fort and could pass the sentry unchallenged. He was always carrying goods of one kind or another. The Mohawks would have to transact their trades outside the walls, but Nathan Beeman would be accompanied all the way into the courtyard, past the well, and meet his prospective customers there. Today he was trading some fish that a man across the lake had caught. Emily could hear the process going on with Captain De la Place himself negotiating the deal

"Beeman, you drive a hard bargain." The Captain allowed a slight grin to form as he admired the vinegar the young man showed in carrying on his business. This time Nathan had asked for gunpowder, which brought De la Place himself down to authorize such a trade.

"Are you sure this powder is just for the local hunters? You wouldn't be handing it over to the Green Mountain Boys, now — would you?"

Captain De la Place stood back a half step to notice the reaction to his question. "We can't be too careful, can we, boy?"

"No, sir. Not when there's those outlaws out there beating up on the King's agents and defying the laws of the Crown. No, as I have told you, sir, if I ever hear of where they are or what they're up to, I would head straight here to tell. For a few gold coins, that is, to keep my mum in a nice new shawl I'd like to buy in Hartford." Nathan gave a slight bow to De la Place and his best smile." I trade for many suppliers along these lake shores. I wouldn't want anything to disturb them or me, Captain."

That afternoon, Emily and Nathan joined hands where the star-shaped top walk of the fort formed a point. He may have been a woodsy, un-soaped lad, but she thought his experience in the woods around Lake Champlain to be exhilarating. Yet she was startled when she heard his words that day.

"Beware of any sudden appearance of hostility, my sweet girl. You have scores of cannons down below. There are thousands of Indians within ten miles of here. Who knows who might appear at that gate with more arms than your company of 40-some men? Do you hear? This is not the place to be for a young lass." His eyebrows arched together over his eyes as if begging her to read between the lines.

"Maybe they would rescue me from this hellish place, Nathan. I want to see dear old London again and have a proper bringing up. I long to hear singing, not the loud voice of that

Mohawk warrior Hendrick and the like. I want to dance in a ballroom, not watch soldiers do a jig in the courtyard. And I want the finery of a dining room table with silk on the place setting, not eating what happens to be the delivery that day. No offense." Emily gave a weary smile.

"None taken, my lady. Who knows what may happen? Just take care of your graceful self and keep an ear out when the geese grow quiet. Your room up yonder is the best place for you if there is any sign of a fight."

Nathan's eyes grew serious. It wasn't quite a warning but a prediction. She had never seen him so intent on a message in the months she had been at the fort. This was different from his tales of travel and deer hunting. He touched her hand once more and walked down the wooden staircase to the courtyard. As he reached the gate, he turned and smiled, tipping his fur cap to Emily. She thought she would never see him again.

Later that evening, her father sat reading a paper at the table. Her mother was near the hearth knitting. She was working on a "silencer, " a thick piece of circular wool that would keep the lid of the commode from slamming shut and alerting anyone that the privy was in use. It reminded Emily further of the discomfort of this place.

"Damn, the man!" Her father picked up the Gazette newspaper and thrust it into the air as if he were picking up a trapped rodent. "Ethan Allen is raving again—saying all this territory west of New Hampshire, this Verdmont, is spoken for in grants authorized in Connecticut. What does that matter, I ask you—when this is the King's land from the Atlantic to the Ohio Territory? The audacity! He dares to proclaim this separate from the Crown? All those cabins springing up east of the lake must be reined in. The inhabitants educated as to their loyalty and their taxes."

Emily sat down and drew close to her father.

"This paper is a week old, father. Where do you think this Allen is now? Is he a violent man?"

"My lass, I neither want to alarm nor keep you from the truth. You and your mother have been very brave here in this, the Empire's outpost. I would like nothing more than to bring you both home safely on His Majesty's ship after our duty is done. But you've never seen a man tied up, smeared with hot tar, covered with feathers from the local fowl, and administered by the local revolutionaries. He's then pointed in the direction of Albany, almost eighty miles to the southwest, relieved of his horse and told to deliver this message of impudence. Fine British agents have died in the freezing forest just trying to do their job." His face grew red with barely contained rage.

"Father, have you seen this yourself?" Emily knew that very few troops ever left the stone walls of Ft. Ticonderoga. Could be a tall tale.

"No, my lamb, but Captain De la Place, who's been in this region longer than I have, has witnessed this torture. And Allen is the man who stirs the pot around here. He's brute enough to assault our agents and wit enough to write about it here in these New England papers." He slammed the paper down, got up from the table, and stood at the window overlooking the now-dark waters of Lake Champlain.

Emily picked up the paper her father had folded to make a better slam on the table. She was a good reader thanks to Madame De la place, but she was not as interested in reading so much as seeing the drawing of a bonnet. It rested near the bottom of the page, an invitation to a shop in Skenesborough, where there were other niceties for young ladies. Or at least an office from which to order one from Boston, she figured

There must be young ladies walking around the small town in pairs, coyly dodging the admiring glances of the local men. Their large winter dresses and colorful fur hats would be a grand sight. Emily fantasized about the steps to the Virginia Reel, a dance a soldier had shown her. But enough! Her happiness will be entwined only with a safe return to the home her family had left only six months ago. When will this service be completed?

Not always did the British army travel with its families and loved ones, but it was an extra benefit for such an unpleasant task in the colonies of America. The King had to offer just a bit more to enlist the kind of professional he needed to defeat the rebellion. At this moment, though, Emily thought nothing of defeat or victory. She only wanted to re-board the ship that sailed her and her parents through the St. Lawrence Seaway and the smaller one that delivered them through the waters of Lake Champlain and to this jutting piece of land on which Ft. Ticonderoga stood.

Thoughts of proper carriages, powdered wigs, and high-button shoes consumed her as she picked up the leather bellows and blew the grey coals of the fire bright red again. Would her father forgive her for feeling this way, she wondered. She would like to ignite her immediate future the same way instead of wasting away on the frontier.

She saw Mt. Defiance looming on the opposite shore through her window. Nathan told her it was named after an Indian girl who refused the advances of a French officer around the time that Ft. Ti was built. As he approached her near the top of the mountain, she threw herself down to a bloody end near the shores of the lake.

Who would come to her aid if the fort were attacked? Would Father be at the ramparts with his cannoneers? Would Nathan be the one to save her if an invasion took place? He was a gritty and determined young man whose manner was crude, his breath like a dog's, and he could neither read nor write. Yet the combination of his strong hands and his soft smile were things she would miss about this place. She climbed into her bed, jutting from the wall, and imagined her family bringing Nathan back across the Atlantic as their servant.

"Oh, I can't bear it. They would laugh him out of Derbyshire," she thought. "Why am I thinking this way? I DO need some rest. "She finally drifted away.

The night enveloped her, and her wonderings melted into a deep sleep. Emily dreamed of a swan, one that would lift her and fly her over the lake and its breaking ice. It was a white bird with wings that looked like the robe of an English reverend when they were extended, and it would call out with glee as she giggled. The beautiful bird would blurt out a regal honking as Emily, dangling in its strong beak over the dark, cold land, felt a joy she hadn't known before. It was the joy of freedom. Slowly the feeling subsided, and all went quiet and blank. Then "BANG!" A shot rang out in the early morning chill with muffled sounds of boots scraping the uneven stones in the courtyard. The sound aroused those along the family quarters on the upper tier inside Ft. Ticonderoga, and doors opened to a shocking sight.

In the face of the morning sun came a huge throng of armed woodsmen walking boldly through the woods of the Green Mountains to the east of Lake Champlin. Their long rifles pointed in every possible direction and covered every square inch of the British bastion with the barrels searching for an unwelcome movement. Father jumped out of bed and into his uniform in the wink of an eye. Outside the door he stood shoulder to shoulder with Captain De la Place. Emily peered into the dark gathering below as wild-looking men poured through the gate of the fort.

He turned and whispered intently, "Get back, Emily. Stay inside and shut the door! Do as I say." He was still slipping an arm into a sleeve as the Captain stood, fists balled up and jammed into his side, his legs parted and his voice indignant from the second floor landing.

"And on whose authority is this?" he bellowed as the masses in leather and fur approached. A quiet intensity held the scene until one man walked swiftly up the wooden stairway and stopped just ten feet from where the commander stood in defiance. The man in deerskin stood over six feet tall, and his eyes flew wide open. His mouth exploded with the words, "In the name of Jehovah and the Continental Congress!"

His rifle was staring at the Captain, eye to eye. With the door to the family's quarters open, Emily looked out as Mother came up behind her. They hunched down slightly and saw the mountain man standing straight as a huge pine tree. Beside him stood a man dressed in stark contrast. A very military-looking man stood in white breeches and a blue jacket with a tricornered hat complete with a feathery plume and golden epaulets on his shoulders. He pointed a silver-plated pistol at the Captain's midsection. But the biggest shock was standing one step below the landing of the first two men. Behind the leaders of this frightening force, who had just taken away a piece of the English Crown, bobbed the head of a young man. Nathan Beeman tried to calm his voice as he announced, "Captain De la Place, and Mr. Smythe, meet General Ethan Allen of the Green Mountain Boys and Colonel Benedict Arnold of the Continental Army!"

Emily quickly closed the door and leaned her back against it. "Mother, it's Nathan! He's been a spy all along. Every day he came to help feed those who welcomed him, and now he aids those who would put a bullet into my father! What treachery!"

She was gasping now, and her mother's arms reached around her in a fearful hug. "What is to become of us now?" Emily's tears erupted as they fled out the back stairwell to the stables to find a driver.

It wasn't until halfway to Hartford that Emily could talk. She and her mother were riding with Mrs. De la Place and a dozen other "dependents," women and children from the fort, who were being sent back East. The wagon they rode was not the most accommodating. It squeaked annoyingly. It seemed as if they hit every bump in the narrow road for the last twenty miles.

"Do you think Father will be all right, Mother?" Emily asked.

"He'll be in Boston soon, Dear, and he'll continue to be a soldier, whether a prisoner—or not." She kept her lips stiff as she spoke and showed neither shame nor fear. "After all, there is no war yet. Possibly he'll be reassigned to a more secure post and won't have to stare down the barrel of a Vermonter's hunting gun." She gathered the large shawl she had knitted around herself and Emily.

Mrs. De la Place, staring straight ahead, said, "Ladies, we are headed in the right direction. A large ship in the harbor awaits, and in a few weeks' time, we'll be in dear old London town. God's will must guide our men 'til we see them again."

Emily thought of Nathan and how he, too, must be part of that great design, God's will. At first, she thought his actions to be that of the devil. But now, on her way back eventually to civilization, she couldn't help but sense that Nathan was on the righteous side of this conflict. She also hoped Father would realize a whole nation of young Nathans was forming and that God's plan included her father's returning across the great Atlantic before he felt their rising fury.

Questions

1. What is the best description of where the Fort is?
   A. In New York State
   B. Near Albany, New York.
   C. In New England
   D. On the New York/Vermont border

2. Why was Emily and her mother patient about their position in life?
   A. The King forced them to be in New York.
   B. They were ready for new adventures in the Colonies.
   C. They wanted Father to get his promotion.
   D. They were not afraid he might be sent into combat.

3. Does this story take place
   A. Before the Revolutionary War?
   B. During the Revolutionary War?
   C. During the War of 1812?
   D. After the Revolutionary War?

4. How does the reader know that Ethan Allen is a worthy
   enemy of the British?
   A. He has a town named after him.
   B. He has a reward posted for his capture.
   C. His writing has been in the newspaper.
   D. He has threatened the British.

5. What word best describes the takeover of the Fort
   A. treacherous
   B. well-planned
   C. imagined
   D. violent

In a paragraph, write how you feel if war separated you from
your family.

Into The Heat

History Lives in our Nation's Parks

Hot? This was really hot. This June in New Jersey was almost as hot as that fire in the old blacksmith's barn Benjamin Miller put out with his father's help last fall. Nelly, the pig knocked the hot coal bucket across the floor, while Mr. Smith was taking his nap. The straw went up fast. After the horses were let out, the two ran for water. But before the neighbors came to save a part of the building, they felt the heat of hell.

Now the boy was carrying water for another purpose. As Washington's army chased the British across the county, the water wagons were farther away than a thirsty soldier could reach. Benjamin thought he had muscles before, but by the time this summer was over, he could lift a horse. His father would tell him, "Fifteen is still too young to carry a musket, Benji, but sergeant Riley says you can carry water for the militia anytime. Just remember to "walk small." As soon as you hear the first shot and you've got empty buckets, do the small walk to cover," Mr. Miller said as he demonstrated. His torso bent close to the polished floor of the handsome New Jersey log cabin.

"Uh course, if you're headed to the front with full buckets, put 'em down and move out." Benji would listen to every word and respectfully nod his head, but knew deep in his heart that he would do anything for the Revolution, even walking straight up to the firing line with two full 50-pound buckets. He saw Sandy Thomas do it last week when they skirmished against the British outside Camden. He heard that Sandy would turn 16 next week, and he was already drilling for the infantry battalion. Lucky him!

"He's nothing but a big baboon," chimed in Felicity, Benji's younger sister. "He doesn't know what East or West is, let alone what they're all fighting for." She folded her arms in front of her at the table with an indignant "Humph!" Benji knew that Felicity cared for Sandy, regardless of her outward expressions.

Even his mother knew patriots from loyalists. She would use the rough, unfinished side of the huge dining room table when cutting her meats and chopping her vegetables. Then, when her family was ready to eat, she would turn it to the highly polished serving side by rotating it around the iron bar that ran through its support struts. The surface would glisten in the candlelight.

But she would show the opposite side when Uncle Robert, the Tory watchmaker from Philadelphia, came to visit. He would babble on about the family's duty to the Mother Country and how anyone who stood in the way was a traitor to England. Uncle Robert's voice blared over the crunch of his footsteps on the walkway to the house. Although the oaken table was usually set to the polished side, Mrs. Miller would immediately react and turn it to the rough side before he touched the door. It was her way of announcing that his views were not those of the host family. Benji always wondered if Uncle Robert ever realized he was seen as an adversary or did the Millers just enjoy an untamed wood surface in the house of a fine carpenter.

"Boy, don't you run with that rat pack of rabble-rousers? I heard of it on the coach this morning. It'll only lead to you getting hung," his big-bellied uncle would bellow. Having surveyed every bit of food on the table, he would have to reach out far to stab his fork at the roasted quail, and his utensil would have to travel even farther back to his huge mouth to allow the food to drop into the bottomless well of a throat. His jowls would shake at the reception. "His Majesty's soldiers hung two boys just about your age in New York when I was there last week. The coachman said there was a gang of little spies and saboteurs here in Monmouth, too, so be careful about who you spend time with, young Benjamin."

Uncle Robert finished the chewing that had been interrupted by his magisterial advice.

Mr. Miller moved to protect his son. "Robert, you stick to selling fine watches to the King's officers, and I'll make sure my child keeps away from the rebels, not to mention an English noose." His eyes narrowed and flashed a signal of defiance at his brother's intrusion into family matters. Uncle

Robert scraped the end of his emptied fork onto the rough table top and seemed impatient at Mr. and Mrs. Miller.

With a look of contempt at Benji, he finally rose and said, "I came to this uncivilized farm country to be among those in tune with me. The Continental Congress is not complying with His Majesty's demands. I've been forced from my place of business because of these attitudes. Instead, the gangs of revolutionary jackals almost took over Philadelphia, my fair city. Is this world turning upside down?"

His whale of a midsection finally rose above the table height as he stood. "Allow me a night's sleep, dear brother, and I will walk to the tavern tomorrow to catch the next coach to New York, where a Loyalist will be respected."

"No quarrel with that, brother. Here, take this reading upstairs with that large candle holder and help yourself to all that's there." Then Mr. Miller picked up his four-cornered, blue carpenter's hat and smacked the table with it. "Just don't speak in my house of hanging rebels while looking at my boy." The brothers stood facing each other with respect, yet with an immeasurable distance between them.

Benji's father had been neutral about the colonies' right to independence for many years. He had not signed on with the army. He even refused to be in the local militia, the volunteers from Monmouth County. His work as a miller of wood and producing the building materials for half the homes in the immediate area aroused no hard feelings among those who joined or the Redcoats who had purchased his fine wagons.

To ensure his allegiance would not be public, Mr. Miller stayed clear of the Silver Tavern, where the political shouting matches took place. Drinkers and teetotalers alike would proclaim to the world where they stood on every issue under the sun. The voices would bay through the night, a stone's throw from his bedroom. Neutrality had been his family history concerning the conflict with Britain, but his mind was changing.

Over dinner the next night on a warm June evening, Mr. Miller proclaimed, "This fight with the King will cost many lives. Most unfortunately, Benjamin, men we know right here in Monmouth County, will perish. The idea of Liberty moves many men, son. It is too costly for this family to participate. The price is too high."

"But father, we all know that one day this new land will be much too big for England to hold. Why can't it begin now? There is enough support for victory if we just convince those who still fear losing a protector instead of seeing the King as a pickpocket," Benji said. "We could have an army just as fine as the Redcoats. "

Mr. Miller looked over at his son with patient understanding. 'Benjamin, we are English. My father, rest his soul, was born there. They have protected us from the Indians, the French, and sometimes from ourselves. Even though their demands seem unfair, we should resolve these issues in a court or Congress. Not on a bloody battlefield."

Wise beyond his years, the boy was exposed to a whirl of ideas from Miss Applegate at school. He knew that the British were on their way back to New York because negotiations had failed in Philadelphia. War was inevitably the only way to settle the conflict now. The Continental Congress would not yield to the taxing policies. Would his father yield to this logic and join the rest of his family in opposing England and supporting the war effort?

June in New Jersey might find Benji and sometimes his sister bringing water and salt pork to the soldiers of the Continental Army. Since the march of the British became known, General Washington gathered a multitude of troops in the colonies in and around Mercer and Monmouth Counties. The mission, so far as Benji heard it, was to attack at the heels of General Clinton's Redcoats until the 12-mile-long column of soldiers, camp followers, and loyalists leaving Philadelphia stopped and held a position. By then, it was hoped that American forces could dominate and unleash the unpredictable damage these soldiers had been so long hoping for.

One morning Benji heard a "Thud" near his window of the house. "Come on out, Benjamin. The day is here!" It was Sandy Thomas, and he was breathless with a loud, yet, whispering voice. "Colonel Morgan's Rangers need us over by the Tennent Courthouse!"

As Benji put on his breeches, he wondered if he should wake Felicity. She would be furious when she found out he had left her behind. But the Rangers were some of the best fighters in the army and would be the first to fire against the British. It's best that she help after all the smoke settles.

As the sun began to rise over the trees of Cranbury, it was already warm. The hamlet was only a short ride to Freehold, where General Cornwallis had just waltzed into the day before.

"They've taken down the church bell at St Peter's in town," Sandy said, "and the locals are forming up, Benjamin. There's bound to be some killing today. The Colonel's gonna need water from the wells to follow up those cannoneers. And that's us."

Sandy was assessing Benji's clothing from top to bottom as he blurted out the information. There must be nothing but approval when they showed up at Morgan's position, ready to water the troops. This might be the biggest day in their lives.

As they turned to run toward their destiny, a stern, booming voice called out, "Benjamin Miller! Come back here." Awkwardly, the boy returned the few yards to stand before his father. "Son, I know I'm not going to stop you from what's going to happen today. Just remember, we are all doing what we think is right." Benji, for the first time, wondered how his very own father would do nothing as he and Sandy served the men who were risking their lives for liberty

" And do the 'small walk' when you see the smoke rise from the British guns. "

They gave each other a man's hug, Benji kissed him on the cheek, and the boys scampered into the woods. Soon they came upon a company of men dressed in blue jackets with rested horses near a stream.

"Sandy Thomas, get to the doctor's tent and present yourselves." A sergeant was waving them to a large canvas construction that would be a field hospital. Inside, a bespectacled, thin man was nervously rubbing his hands together when not clattering utensils down on wood-planed tables. He was preparing for the wounded.

"Boys, the King's Cold Stream Guards just marched out of Freehold with a fife and bagpipe escort. Cornwallis won't take kindly to what General Lee and Lafayette are planning for him. There will be plenty of work today, I can tell you."

The doctor seemed unusually calm until two more men walked in with boxes of medicine. He finally exhaled and said, "Ah, Walker, Jones, these are the boys I was telling you about," glancing suspiciously at Benji, whom he had never seen before. 'Now, Thomas, we don't know if this place will be overrun in the middle of an operation or stay quiet and unused for the remainder of the month, but I want one of you to stay here at all times. We may have to carry these boxes out of here if the enemy arrives before our wounded. And we will not allow this stuff to fall into British hands. Understand?"

Sandy looked at Benji, and both nodded back at the doctor. They located two big wooden buckets in the tent, walked over, and gave them a lift as the men returned to stocking the tent. Just then, a commotion arose as the cavalry contingent suddenly mounted outside. The men in the tent opened the flap with anxious expressions. Benji felt his heart starting to race.

"Sandy, how do you tell the sound of British horses from American horses inside this tent?" The men walked outside.

The older boy motioned toward the bottom of the canvas facing the noise, and they both peered out into the sunlight. The three-dozen men with long rifles raised alongside their Jersey-breed steeds exploded onto a field and up toward a rise. There on the top could be seen the pride of the Colonial Army, the artillery of George Washington facing down toward the opposite hill, poised for an eruption.

"They're pointing toward Mr. Carr's house, Benji. I hope they don't blow him and the family up," Sandy said breathlessly.

"Oh, they're long gone, Sandy. Mr. Carr, quiet as it's kept, is a member of the militia. He'll probably be with his unit over at the Tennent Church." Benji gritted his jaw tight and whispered softly, " I wished to God my father was with him."

"Don't take it so hard, Benji. At least he's not running as your uncle did. He'll come around before long."

"He told me he was delivering some windows to Briar Hill today like nothing was goin' on. Heck, I heard a column ten miles long is headed this way. He doesn't even let that affect business. It's awful flusterin', I'll tell ya. " The boy lowered his head and smacked the tent with his open hand.

Benji picked up an empty water bucket and stood next to the tent's opening.

"Let's see if we can find some action, Sandy. We can't wait here 'til the end of the war."

Despite their order to stay put, the boys set out for Middletown Road, where the main body of the English was bound to be marching sometime this day. Even though the morning dew would create a lush scene, the heat of the Monmouth County farmland was upon them. Their buckets bounced against their legs as they struggled to reach high ground. Colonial troops should occupy the hill, but it now lay empty. Disappointed, Benji and Sandy trudged up and down the hills. Into a patch of woods toward the path of the British, they scurried. The only sound was the dull knocking of the buckets against their legs. As the boys marched through the trees, cannon fire could finally be heard in the distance.

Benji looked at his more experienced friend with an apprehensive expression.

"Is this as far as we go? The surgeon said not to wander off in case we're needed back there, and where is there a well around here anyway, Sandy? Seems like we're stretchin' ourselves too thin."

'Now look, do you want to provide water for them boys to shave with back at the tent, or do you want to see the Colonial Army knock the hell out of the Redcoats?"

Sandy started to climb a small rise, and Benji, bucket flapping, followed him. "Aw, I'm with ya, but I can feel that steamin' heat, and the men will be calling for us somewhere soon." Benji looked around and saw men dressed in green uniforms with "Virginia" patched on the arm. As they rose to the top of a hill, soldiers were wearing the blue jackets of the army with "Third Pennsylvania" inscribed on the sleeve. These men were from all over the continent. On the top of this hill, a long line of cannons and cannoneers proved that a battle of historic proportions was imminent.

The boys could see the 15 or so guns facing straight out over a newly plowed field where the waves of heat were rising, and through them, the Americans could see the British emplacement. They had turned round from their route to Sandy Hook and a voyage to New York to teach the rebels a lesson—a small "engagement" then back to the big city.

"General Stirling," a man shouted, "we'll take a range here. We're dead set on the opening in the trees where the column has to go. They'll be like ducks on a pond, sir."

Benji and Sandy saw the glint of iron from the weapons on the rise fifty yards away. As he looked around, he saw the patches on the uniforms and noticed men from Massachusetts and even Georgia. If these men were here at this crossroads in time, why wasn't his father? Was he afraid of battle? Did he not care enough for this new country? Why wasn't he loyal enough to the colonies he made a living from to risk being here? These were questions he never dared to ask him

As these thoughts began to recede, *BANG*, the first shots, went off right in front of his face. Just 20 yards away, the artillery line began its succession of explosions, and he and Sandy ran farther up the hill to get a better look. With the water buckets dropped at the bottom of a large tree, they scrambled up for a breathtaking view: scores of square miles of farmland soon to be converted to a battlefield. The burnt gunpowder drifted to their noses as the corn, tomatoes, and cabbage had to wait for attention. Now there was killing to do.

The sound of big guns dominated the New Jersey fields for the next half hour. The sweating artillerymen called for water. The boys ran down to a nearby creek and filled them up continuously. A few British cannonballs had landed nearby, but the worst was a blast that tore up a farmhouse in the distance, yet the screams could be heard all the way up on the boys' hill. At about that time, they saw the woman with the skirt half torn off bringing water up a hill to a neighboring cannon position. How odd she looked, they thought. So determined was she to bring relief to the heated men. Where did she come from, Benji wondered. This was the aptly-named Molly Pitcher. The citizens were coming from all over the colonies to face the Redcoats.

The heat had risen with the sun's arc through the sky, and at about noon, the gunnery sergeant yelled, " The Brits look as if they're trying to move their artillery back, but the horses won't move. They got 'em hitched to the guns, but they're going nowhere." He put the spyglass down on a nearby stump and reached for some greasy beef jerky that slid from a pouch. 'Maybe we can have a bit of a blow ourselves, sir."

A captain nearby stood with his hands on his hips.

"Just a bit of a breather, sergeant. We aren't done with this by a long shot," he warned. "I've heard Washington is riding to our rear and tongue-lashing every man who steps backward even one pace."

"Excuse me, sergeant," Benji pleaded. "Could I have a look through the glass?"

The crusty man hadn't shaved in days. His body hadn't seen a tub or a creek in a long time, and sweat ran down every inch of his worn face. "Sure, lad. Then get us another bucket of water, will you?"

Benji put the metal tube to his right eye and focused on what the men had been firing at. Across the small valley to the other hill, his eye landed on the British gunners still wearing thick red coats. What dedication they must have to be so loyal to their uniform and country. The Hessians, hired soldiers from Germany, were deserting in big numbers, tired of sweltering in the summer of this strange land. But these soldiers were going to do their duty until the end.

Then Benji's eye wandered over to the right, where Middletown Road could be seen through the tree line about a mile away. West of where he was spotting now, the trumpets, fifes, and drums had so recently announced the arrival of the British column. Who knows where the remainder of the thousands on that road this morning are?

Sandy slid up next to his friend on the top of the hill. "Hey, gimme a look there, Private Benjamin!"

"Wait a minute. I don't believe what I see."

Sandy was impatient now and grabbed for the glass.

"Wait, I tell ya. I think I see something that must be one of those mirages in the desert. Take a look just to the right of the stone fence on Middletown Road over yonder." Benji handed the glass to Sandy with his jaw dropped almost to his chest.

Sandy saw the blue tri-cornered hat Benji saw on a man performing some task right next to a buggy with two brightly dressed women. From a distance, it was hard to make out more than that.

"Can you tell me if you think that is who I think that is?" Benji took the glass back and squeezed his eye into the opening as tightly as he could. The man was, in fact, his father! And those dresses were not worn by strangers either.

Sandy sat back with his mouth wide open, "That's your father as sure as the day is long. I thought you said he was just deliverin' today. They're awful near that British column, Benji. Do you think they know that?"

From the boys' perspective on the hill, they could see for miles in any direction. However, no one would know of a hostile force's position from the tree-lined farm roads. And the positions kept changing.

"I've got to get down there and warn them. What the devil are they doing there?"

Benji picked up his bucket and cautiously laid it aside. "Sandy, you stay here for the captain. I've got to run to my father. The rest of that column is bound to show up on that road any minute, and who knows what mood they'll be in."

"But you said he's a fence sitter. He could convince the Brits of his being neutral if he had to, couldn't he?" Sandy was begging his friend not to descend the hill. He had heard of boys hanged for spying. This was getting much too confusing, with the enemy appearing and disappearing. A squad of grenadiers could show up in a moment, the last he would see of dear Benjamin.

"I'll be back just as soon as I find out they're alright." And he walked slowly down the hillside to the left past lines of resting infantrymen. He saw men removing their shirts. The heat was like an oven rising from the rolling countryside. He could recognize the last place he noticed his father, mother, and sister through the waves rippling over the roasting fields. They had been next to a large well on a pasture just off Middletown Road, about a mile away. He would have to walk nimbly not to alarm any soldier or risk being enlisted to perform a duty that would keep him from reaching his family. What if a Colonial grabbed him to go for water?

The other question was, what were his beloved mother and father doing in the middle of such a battle? Could he be that ignorant of the situation? Surely he must have heard the cannon fire. He could not want to deliver a chair that badly. With a determined bite of his lip, Benji thought that his father should not be anywhere but up on that hillside with the

Colonial regiments. Why hadn't he come around by this time to land on the side of the rebels?

It was strange being here trying to warn his own father about danger as he reached the road. The air was burning his lungs as he took a deep breath and looked left and right from beside a huge oak tree. He had seen this mark of the road from the hill and knew they had been here. Again he looked toward the East and saw a puff of dust circling the road. Could it have been his family's wagon? It had taken him fifteen minutes to get there. They might be well on their way. Why had they stopped in the first place? And where were they going? Benji thought his father was working on a bed frame for the Craigs, but that was in the other direction.

Now what? Just return to the hill or try to look further for his family? He decided to trot across the road to the well quickly. As he crossed, he saw it was not as worn as it might have been if the whole ten-mile-long column, artillery and all, had passed this way. The English army would not just run. Most of the Brits would stand to fight the Americans instead of wholesale retreat toward the bay.

But as he peered into the well, he saw that there was one more enemy the Brits had to concern themselves with. As thirsty as this column was to be by the time it made it to this point, this well had been filled up after a morning's march through the summertime swelter! It was crammed with rocks, long planks, and pieces of smaller lumber that made dipping into water impossible. The well was blocked! It would take hours to lift that debris so the enemy would die of thirst first. And now he knew. His father had chosen sides that day.

Benji returned to the hillside in time for the artillery duel. He had been lifted as if a trumpet call was being played next to his ear for days.

This day became the famous Battle of Monmouth, raising the hopes and pride of all the citizens of the Colonies. Although the British made their way back to New York to fight again, the people in Monmouth County realized the Miller family now fought for Washington.

1. Why did Mrs. Miller 'turn the tables' on Uncle Robert?
    A. She was being inhospitable.
    B. To eat fancy food
    C. To insult someone
    D To reverse a situation.

2. How does the reader know that Uncle Robert is not anti-British?
    A. He says, "His Majesty."
    B. He sells watches to anyone.
    C. He tells his brother to be careful for his son.
    D. He leaves Philadelphia.

3. Benji's father:

    A. felt protective and responsible for the safety of his brother.
    B. felt hostility and fear in his son.
    C. felt guilty about his loyalty.
    D. Was beginning to adopt his son's sympathies in the war

4. Who did Mr. Miller sell his wood products to?
    A. Anyone who had his price.
    B. The British

C. The Americans
D. Philadelphians

5. Why was Mr. Miller so quick to respond to his brother's advice?
   A. He thought that it was none of his brother's business.
   B. He was afraid that his brother might turn Benji in for spying.
   C. He thought that his brother should turn rebel.
   D. He didn't want his wife to hear what his brother said.

6. In a paragraph, predict how Mr. Miller will act during the remainder of the Revolutionary War.

Fisherman Two

Francis Scott Key Prepares the National Anthem

In the year 1814, the British armies seemed to cover the world. They occupied most of Canada, recruiting Indians to fight the new country, America. They were in France trying to rein in Napoleon. They were in New Orleans fighting Andrew Jackson and had just come from Washington, where they burned the new Capitol. Now they were coming to Baltimore.

"Father, why do the Redcoats want to take on the whole world?" Gordie frowned as he asked his painful question.

"Just look lively there, Gordon, and make sure those nets are rolled tightly."

Mr. Forman was at the tiller of his boat, "Fisherman Won," and the mackerel were flopping out of the huge barrel balanced in the middle of the 20-foot scow. He tied off the long tiller, which connected to the rudder, with rope looping around it while the ends attached to both sides of the old wooden boat. Then he stood up to grab the main line to drop the sail.

"Got some oysters in here, too," the boy said. "Look good enough to sell."

"You leave the sellin' to me, son. Better you help me roll up the mainsail. And stop lookin' at the horizon now. Those Brits will be here faster than you know. We gotta scoot home before Mother starts to worry."

They pulled up the oars, sat side by side, and muscled the last few yards to shore. Slight waves pushed the boat to the sand, while Mr. Forman thought this might be the calmest around this beach for a while. He pictured the nasty faces of an angry army that soon would be spewing out of the huge British warships.

They pulled the bow up to a large iron loop on the beach, planted far enough to keep the small craft from floating away, and trudged to their cabin with the day's catch. Dragging the fish on a large canvas across the sand, Gordie wondered what he could do against the invaders.

Back at the small shack the Forman's called home, just a short sail from Ft. McHenry, Mother had the fireplace roaring. September was getting chillier here in Baltimore. Mr. Forman could have worked on the larger ships in the harbor but chose to fish independently. He loved his freedom. Some seamen felt the urge to pirate goods from unsuspecting merchants, especially those from Portugal or Spain who sailed in unfamiliar waters. Local men would climb aboard large ships by force, stick a pistol in a captain's face and take off with hands full of valuables or anything they could fit in their fast little runabouts. Then they might raise the flag of the new United States to prevent the local constable from gazing on their ill-gotten gains after sailing back to their maze of inlets and marshes.

Mother chimed in, "Now Gordie, don't get any grand ideas of joining those danged ruffians. You're 14, and that isn't near enough to bein' a man fightin' the British. One of those cannonballs falls on your head. It'd ruin your whole day."

Mr. Forman smiled at his wife's try at humor. Although he knew it was their job to keep Gordie from trouble in all kinds of ways, their poor lives would get much worse if Baltimore was taken. And Admiral Cochrane would show the Americans no mercy as he tried to teach these pirates a lesson at the mouth of the Patapsco River. Then destroy Ft. McHenry itself.

"Father, Terrance, and Pudgy both got on a skiff the other night and saw men throwing hand bombs at the big ships. They sailed away safe with the current, and their good seamanship got them home, laughin' over it. Bet the Brits didn't sleep so easy on board that night." Gordie showed his big pearly teeth with too big a smile for Mother's liking.

"That's exactly what I'm saying. Keep away from those damned pirates," commanded mother, scowling.

"They're not pirates, Mother. They got commissioned by the state of Maryland to defend the coast, so I wouldn't be calling them bad words. They're not stealing. They're giving. Givin' the Brits hell for coming here. They're called the Sea Fencibles."

Mr. Forman closed the evening with a warning. "Those ships are dangerous out there, son. Troops aboard could come this way and bayonet the whole town. They shoot cannonballs that burst into the air and rain down bullets of steel. Better give them leeway and let Major Armstead at Ft. McHenry do what he's supposed to do."

Gordie wasn't convinced. He was a man. Since his family and town faced a terrible invasion, he must find a way to help. Father would never let him take out the Fisherman Won with any of his friends. So what could he do?

"You leave that boat alone, my boy. Don't let any of your ne'er-do-well friends get your ear to mess about with the Redcoats ready to burn us out of house and home." Father warned his son constantly. Mother became more nervous with every passing day.

The next day his father left early to use the seining nets by himself, leaving Gordon to study his letters at home in the grey shingled shack. After putting down his McGuffey Reader, he suddenly slipped out behind Mother's back, down to the beach to scan the horizon. He might be first to see the tall masts of the invading British fleet and warn the town. In the chill of the September morning, he walked through the sand and stood with his boots facing the tiny breaking waves. Then he saw a shape. More than a speck, it stood out in the grey waters of the bay. A small wooden pram of a boat was dawdling, bouncing slightly on the surface, as Gordie peered out. Instantly scanning around him, he saw no one on the boat as it meandered near enough to the shore for him to grab the bow.

Pulling the boat onto shore was a tough task as he hungrily saw the contents of this gift from the sea. One plank across the middle and an attached slab of wood at each end of the eight-foot-long craft showed it was a life raft of sorts, but when he looked under a pile of bailing sponges, he knew where it came from. A box of stick-matches with the likeness of King George on it! Whoa. This lifeboat slipped off one of those big battleships.

"I'm taking this prisoner of war!" Gordie screamed. His buttons almost burst through his well-worn shirt as he stuck out his chest like a warrior. Back home, it didn't go so well.

Father didn't appreciate the capturing of the foreign craft, warning Gordie, "Son, I'm walking off to the Constable's house right now to see what we can do with it. This is not our property. And I don't want you getting us into a pack of trouble here. Mr. Ratliff will know what to do." He picked up the English matchbox and looked around at his wife.

"I'm coming too," Mother cried.

Father turned to leave his son with the boat on the beach, just steps away from their front door, where Gordie had dragged it. A crazy idea crept into the boy's head. These aren't the times for patriots to be good boys. The Redcoats were going to invade Baltimore, the ships would soon be bombing Ft. McHenry, and we'd be speaking the 'King's English" next week. If we don't find the sails of the British soon, the whole harbor will be lit up with bombs bursting in the air.

Gordie took off to the shed, found a long rake handle, then picked up an oil cloth Mother used to cover the table sometimes, as well as some coiled rope. It was his boat now. Like one of the Sea Fencibles, he took over a foreign vessel and now would prepare to meet the enemy. The little boat felt heavy as he slid it over the beach toward the bay. The long narrow skeg dragged behind, digging into the sand. Maybe he should have gotten Terry or Pudgy to help him, but "naw." They'd just slow him down. Make it more complicated. He would sail out to the horizon, be the first to see the mast on the tall ships, and warn the coastline of the battle to come.

He had no oar, so the little breeze would have to do. Late afternoon on the inlet, usually a peaceful time for the coastal folks of Maryland, Gordie's instinct kicked in. Catch a puff of air and go! Soon he was making a wake, making time, and moving his little craft out past the weeded fingers of the bay. The tablecloth sail was holding. He had chopped off the head of the rake, placed the bottom of it between his feet, and now kept it as sturdy as he could, with his right hand holding the main sheet, the roped line, to the corner of the made-up sail. But he felt strong, like the big fisherman down at the docks.

Sailing at an angle to the breeze, he needed to tack a few times, switching positions of the sail, now moving over, with his left arm straining at the line as the tiny boat crept toward the horizon. His grey shingled house became smaller, yet out he went with his homemade seacraft. The spray from the side, still warm from the summer, felt fine, but now the sun was getting low, and a definite chill greeted the late afternoon. But Gordie sailed on.

Then a chilling splash of water jumped up over the high side of the boat and crashed into him, soaking the whole of his clothes. "Should have worn a slicker out here," he thought as the sun went down behind him. As Gordie realized the cold might hold him back from his quest to spy the British before anyone else, he started to tremble. He'd never been out in any boat in the dark without Father. He now was soaked from head to toe as the waves started breaking more frequently into the little boat's hull. Then the rain. The darkening skies seemed to be angry with him, defying his father. Disobeying Mother. But it was all for the Country, the New Country.

As he came about to head home, a giant tree seemed to appear over his left shoulder. *Wait.* Warships began rounding the hook of the Penobscot River and heading his way. Gordie quickened his moves turning and setting his tiny sail toward home. What was he thinking? He could never get close to these huge ships. Spot them he could, but now they were bearing down on him like a bear chasing a dog. A slow dog. Now settling in as he sailed downwind, he realized the tide rolling with the waves was behind him and pushing him toward shore. Up with one wave, then down. Then up again with another swell behind and down again. The motion felt like the time he was sledding up north with his cousins in New York. His hand firmly on the tiller connected to the small rudder that kept on course, he felt fear for the first time.

The wind grew loud, but he could see cabin lights in the distance. He thought he heard a cannon shot. WHOOOM! One ship lit up as its big guns shot westward toward the fort. Gordie spied men standing on the decks as the one ship crept closer. BOOM! Another ship beyond the nearest started blasting too. He wondered how close they were to the American troops on shore. Were the big guns in range of the Fort? Suddenly, he saw the nearby ship fire another round which seemed to be from a smaller cannon. He turned to see the letters, W-O-L-V-E-R-I-N-E light up as the shot screamed through the air. *Faster. I have to go faster than the waves are pushing. Pull in that sail.* He darted to the left downwind but was now more open to the waves as they pounded the craft at more of an angle. WHOOMP! WHOOMPPP! Two shots now. One from a third vessel started to open up its huge cannons. He now thought he, too, was dodging the shots as the bombardment of Baltimore had begun. The bombs bursting in air. *Please get me home!*

His father screamed as the little bow scraped the sandy beach. "Gordie, you silly boy. Get the hell in here!"

Mother was standing right next to him as her face lit up with another volley from the British toward the shoreline a mile away.

"We told you not to go out there," she wailed. "Just get out of that thing and in the house."

Gordie shivered as he took the bow line, and his father pulled down the makeshift mast and sail. As soon as they had the boat in tow and safely held on the beach, Mr. Forman picked up the sail to roll it up and noticed it wasn't a sailcloth but an oilcloth that Mother used for the table!

"Wait. What's this?" he cried.

Gordie leaned over to see what Father saw on his sail. As Mother leaned in, she whimpered, "Oh, my God! It's been cannon shot!"

Mr. Forman stuck his whole arm through a ten-inch gash in the sail and wriggled his fingers.

"This should have been you. Boom, another casualty in his tiny boat near his mother's house."

Mother looked closer. "This must have just buzzed past that empty skull of yours. Luckily, it wasn't one of those exploding bombs. We'd be picking up your pieces in the water."

"Get inside now, and we'll make some stew," Mr. Forman said.

Gordie humbled, stumbled along the beach toward the house, then stopped. He hadn't heard or felt that cannon shot pierce his sail with the rain pouring down.

"Father, which flag did you see when you went to the Fort?"

"The American battle flag," his father said.

Gordie looked up at his father with a painful grin.

"Will it be there in the morning?"

"I don't know, son. They have just begun to fight."

1. What was the biggest reason for the War of 1812?
    A. British wanted to end slavery.
    B. They thought the Revolutionary War wasn't finished.
    C. It was a conflict for dominance over the seas.
    D. They needed more training with weapons.

2. What is surprising about the kind of bombs they used?
    A. They burst in the air.
    B. They were made of plastic.
    C. They were very colorful.
    D. They were made in the Colonies.

3. Why did Gordie have a "painful grin"?
    A. He was wounded.
    B. He was sad about Baltimore.
    C. He was proud and afraid at the same time.
    D. He was embarrassed.

4. Why did Gordie's father wonder if the flag would be there the next day?
    A. Someone might steal it.

B. He didn't know if the Americans would win.
C. He thought that it might be too damaged.
D. The flagpole might have fallen.

What might be a good reason for disobeying your parents?

While Waiting Wharfside

Lewis and Clark at the Columbia River

"Doesn't anyone recognize us?" Mr. Thompson asked aloud. The harbormaster surely remembers Mr. Lewis, the well-dressed gentleman who looked then like an Eastern-bred politician. And he must recall Lieutenant Clark, the large red-headed man with a stiff military back. These were not the same boats the men left in, but someone should realize who these men were. After being away for so long and dreaming of a return to warm beds and a civil meal, they'll have to spend another night on this barge of boards. It was well after sundown, and the Lewis and Clark expedition was exhausted. The Corps of Discovery had come home.

The wharf was dark, but Thompson, the chronicler and First Mate of this long journey, could see the dockworkers throwing their arms in the air. They look like huge, dark birds fighting over a piece of meat. Someone said the shoremen needed to get paid before docking this group of strangers. Who were these odd-looking visitors, some dressed in bear skins, walrus hide, or headwear from wolf fur?

"Don't you leave that pile uh junk here! And that other raft behind you is about to sink." The dock worker curled his lip and turned his back, slowly walking away.

Indeed the second barge supported only two men and the last of the supplies, so Merriweather Lewis ordered it sunk as soon as he and Lt. Clark got each man a bed in town.

Thompson shouted in disdain, "Our two leaders have left to get your fees," He wondered if Lewis and Clark had enough credit anywhere in town. The men of the Expedition hadn't seen American money since they left the Pacific ocean. Silver, gold, and animal pelts were the coin of the day.

"How outrageous! We are returning to St. Louis after two and a half years of exploration for our country, and we can't tie up because we have no money?" Thompson snorted."

The outline of the city looked different. Now in the chilly September evening, he could see buildings almost as tall as some of the mountains they had just come from. The Rockies, the Sierras, and the Cascades stuck in his mind. The government probably thinks they're dead since no word had returned from Washington in a year. And unreliable messengers from the wilderness may not have arrived there at all. But not another night on this freezing boat!

Just a few days ago, there was talk of when the Expedition might arrive at the port and how there might no longer be the same authorities in the city as when they left. But all the men could think of was touching that wharf. Oh, what a welcome they'd receive! Think of the meats, pies, jams, and candies. That's what they missed while meandering through this forlorn country. Eating rabbits, squirrels, roots, and insects was over. It's hard to believe that anyone would want to live out there.

The two dozen men were looking so expectantly toward every morning, feasting on hope. The usual gloom had faded. Surely they accomplished a lot. The first white men to be in all these places, from the Mississippi River to the Pacific Ocean, while Thompson and Mr. Lewis wrote the experiences down. Descriptions of thousands of plants and trees never described before would be seen by the best scientists in the United States. The tales of contact with the Indian tribes of the Missouri Valley and the Mandans of the Dakotas would be envied by all those who could read. Clark, the big soldier from Virginia, and Lewis, the moody genius who used to be Thomas Jefferson's secretary, should be famous forever. If only they could get home in one piece.

That was a matter of some doubt on at least a few occasions. The first winter was spent eating boiled roots, candles, and dogs. Boots had worn through so they wore rags around their feet to keep them warm. Many men became sick in unsanitary conditions. The diet was so repetitious. Corn mush in the morning, corn fritters at noon, and corn cakes for supper. There were weeks and weeks of tasteless stuff one wouldn't look twice at in St. Louis. Heck, there you walk a dog, you don't eat it!

And then there was Chief Twisted Hair and his warriors who wanted to kill the invaders, but instead, he let the Corps build a fort right across from their village. Lewis and Clark survived the winter there, and in the spring, went off further in search of a passage to the Pacific. They ate wildflowers and roasted tree bark when the designated hunters couldn't find food. They spent months sleeping and shivering under the stars. Everyone was sick to death at one time or another. One did die. But "Thank God," Thompson thought, that's all. It very easily could have been him.

He was 22 now and started out just as a hired hand to help with the supplies, yet he had no idea he'd have to pull the big rafts up the rivers. What work! The writers, artists, and mapmakers weren't assigned to do the muscle work against the strong current like the big boy Brady. But there were times when even he had to get out and pull.

America would know a lot more about this continent than it knew before. They were the Corps of Discovery, yet they all wondered if anyone would remember them. It looked right then as if nobody cared at all. It was night, and very few lamplights were still lit in buildings around the docks.

Suddenly another figure came forward out of the darkness. "Is this your crew here? Ha! Looks to me like you're a bunch of Frenchies lookin' for a free handout. What's the matter, then? The Indians didn't get a fair shake with ya?" An older dock hand now approached the exhausted congregation of explorers.

"We were sponsored by the government in Washington. We've done Jefferson's bidding, and now we are served disrespect instead of roast meats," Thompson retorted. "Our Captain Mr. Clark and Mr. Lewis have gone to fetch some currency at the nearest hotel, but that could take some time."

Another dock hand hovered nearby with a well- lit torch to help the investigation. Those who had been asleep now arose from flattened bed rolls and looked out into the blackness toward the light. Too weary to feel the joy of being home, they listened to still more surliness from the shoreman's companion, who also seemed to disbelieve the First Mate's story.

"Everybody that comes to this dock in St Louis is on a schedule. And at this time in the evening, I know there is no time table you are respecting. My orders are not to tie up anyone who is not scheduled—and that includes you gentlemen! Harbormaster's orders."

Thompson looked across from the docking area and saw huge riverboats with masts disappearing into the sky to make the run to New Orleans. Those sailors are fast asleep in warm beds, and our esteemed leaders are listening to an uncouth slug who has no right to tell them they must sleep at anchor after two years of sacrifice.

The men now missed Brady as they anticipated landing. He'd been missing too long. They tried to make him a cook, but he burned the biscuits every time he tried. The young man was barely twenty, and Lewis and Clark felt guilty for recruiting such a youth. After looking Brady's mother in the eye, they felt a twinge of guilt as he said "goodbye" to his dog and the only home he ever knew. He did have a decent horse and proved he was skillful with a knife which could come in handy. Plus, he could read. One of the goals of the Corps of Discovery was to make maps of the Louisiana Territory, which had just been added to the newly incorporated states, to the Pacific Ocean, or wherever else they might wind up. Writing descriptions of the countryside, the types of tree growth, and the size of the mountains while naming the regions no white man had seen, required a certain sense of literacy.

Why had they let him out of their sight? Days ago, he went off to search for a rabbit or two he could trap. Hunger filled most of the explorers' days. Brady also had a feel for Indian languages. The woman Sacajawea took a liking to him and taught him some of her native Shoshone tongue. Although most Northern Plains Indians were constantly at war with other tribes, the Shoshone peacefully roamed the flat country following buffalo herds. Sacajawea chose to follow a Frenchman who traded in pelts and furs. Because he often spent many days away looking for business, she felt free enough to go off alone. She met up with Lewis and Clark in what is now North Dakota riding her bareback horses thousands of miles to join their amazing travels. Young Brady was the handsomest of the group, so she spent more time with him sharing languages, cooking methods, and the love of the outdoors.

But now here were Lewis and Clark, having returned from a two-year journey as the Corps of Discovery found themselves without proper identification or money. But Brady carried their paperwork, their commission from President Jefferson. And he was missing in action. Or was he? Suddenly the sound of horses filled the quiet docks.

"Brady, where in the Sam Hill you been?" Thompson spouted out.

Casually riding up to the wharf from a stand of trees came two horsemen. Brady started to belly laugh in his saddle, which showed a couple of dangling rabbits bouncing from the side of his steed. The other rider had long black hair, dark eyes, and copper-colored skin. As the horse trotted forward toward the men and their rafts, the white teeth of an Indian woman flashed with a bright glow.

"Sacajawea too. We thought you ran away together."

She dismounted with pride in her stance and said, "Found boy looking for food. Didn't know how close he was to city. We have cow steak tonight, no?" She chuckled as she looked over the exhausted men. "After long ride, hungry." She smiled deeply.

Brady offered, "She needs a medal and a meal."

Thompson filled Brady in on the distressing particulars. The city of St. Louis was not ready for them. They might have to wait until business hours in the morning before any banks opened up to present the commission papers and get enough money to land the Expedition. At any rate, nobody was going to put up two dozen men, and now one woman, who just climbed out of the wilderness if they just knocked on a door. There'd be no place to sleep but right there on the rafts, once again looking up at the stars.

Sacajawea never flinched. "I sleep like always. Next to my horse. Brady, you on the boat." She laughed.

It would be one more night before America welcomed the party of Lewis and Clark.

1. How does the reader know that at least one of the party is a
   military man?
   A. There is an extremely large man.
   B. One was wearing a uniform.
   C. He is named Lieutenant Clark.
   D. He carries a musket.

2. What is meant by a "civil meal"?
    A. One that is not made up entirely of corn.
    B. One with civilized company
    C. A quick bite to eat.
    D. One provided for by the government.

3. What was Thompson doing away for two and a half years?
    A. He was banished to the wilderness.
    B. He was in the army.
    C. He was spying on the Indians.
    D. He was exploring and mapping the country.

4. How did Thompson describe the men on the docks?
    A. sneaky
    B. hungry
    C. bird-like
    D. sleepy

5. What would be the next thing, besides a good meal, that
    one of the men would want?
    A. A barber
    B. A chaplain
    C. New shoes
    D. A bed

6. In a paragraph, write what you would have done if you
    were Lewis or Clark, and compare it with a time your
    good deed was not recognized immediately. What did
    you do?

The Book of Life

Two Armies - One Country

Bobby Hannah had seen a million men come through his small town. He wasn't quite sure how many a million was, but it had to be at least that. They all had fresh horses, good boots, and uniforms with no patches at all. They were the Union army, and he wondered why the men from his town usually looked like they had stepped out of a trash barrel. Most of them had already left. The Civil War didn't care where men were from as long as they were willing to die for their side.

His family, one of the few that stayed while the invasion took place, called it an invasion because these men sure weren't from Maryland. There was his baby brother Liam who couldn't travel well, they said. Of course, how would they know he couldn't travel well if he never did it? What if he was only a year old? He guessed they would have to wait until Pa got home from Richmond or the war was over, whichever happened first. His mother would have them pray every night for his safe return. At any rate, they had to stay and watch all these Northerners move on through his neighborhood to set up camp outside his town.

Toby didn't like 'em either. He was the black boy Mr. Hannah said should amount to somethin', even if there is slavery in the Confederate States of America. Paw hated slavery, but there was much more to this war than the sin of involuntary servitude. Nevertheless, Toby was real smart, and Bobby always asked him what he thought about things.

"Ah, hate dem bluebellys. Yessah, Ah hate 'em. Ah know they supposed to free my people," Toby was holding court, "but meanwhile they kilt a whole lot a men ah know'd."

The two boys were standing on a hollowed-out log near Keedysville, Maryland, in 1862, and war surrounded them.

Toby wasn't allowed to go to school, so Bobby had to bring his books home every night. Mrs. Morris, the school marm, didn't think Bobby was using those books at home. He would read to his black friend, and then Toby would read it back. Mrs. Hannah had to look the other way when she saw the two boys together because a book would always be in Toby's hand. She told Mrs. Morris she wished it were her boy who liked to read so much.

The thing that kept Toby out of school was the Slave Codes. And even though Toby's family was free, you didn't advertise anywhere in the South that you were teaching black people to read.

"14-year-old boys should be fishin'," Bobby's mother would say, wanting them to be less conspicuous with the books. So that's what they did. They took their fishing poles **and** their books over to the creek and would read a popular book titled *Uncle Tom's Cabin* or *Life Among the Lowly*. Toby thought they wrote the book about his father; it was so close to his real life.

The sky was a funny gray with patches of blue scattered between the clouds. "Look," Toby said, "We got the blue and the gray up in the sky. Which one's gonna take over? The blue sky or the gray clouds?"

"You mean like the uniforms? blue and gray?" Bobby could count on Toby to be observant. "I wonder when they're gonna fight around here. Looks like they're fixin' to do somethin' with all those cannons over by the peach farm."

The black boy would read the papers from town, and his father was privy to the conversation from the soldiers when he sold his turnips at the roadside stand. "They say that General Lee himself is comin' up from Richmond for this one. That's what Paw says."

One morning a few days later, the boys realized the peace was about to change. The soldiers did not leave camp to buy food from the local farmers this September day, and a strange silence accompanied the dawn. Bobby would not go to school now that they felt something was about to erupt. At a brisk pace, they made their way up to the fields where the camp was said to be. They had to be the first to know.

Toby had climbed up above Bobby on a small incline in the woods. He figured they would be able to see the fields that were adjacent to the bluebellys' encampment. As Bobby scrambled up next to him, Toby peered over the top and gasped. He sighted 10,000 fighting men preparing for battle.

Though battalions of men were gearing up, they were obscured by the treeline of poplars with dark green summertime leaves. "Yup. There they are!" They, officially, were behind enemy lines.

Bobby craned his neck to see too. "Whadya think they're up to, Toby?"

"Ah 'spect they about to charge after the first sight of gray uniforms and not stop 'til either side is all dead."

His friend spoke matter-of-factly. Toby was not impressed by the number of Union Army regulars. The newspapers called them the Army of the Potomac. With the clean uniforms, shiny rifles, and huge cannons, he wanted them gone from the land his family loved.

Just as he was wondering this, BOOM, the loudest sound Toby or Bobby had ever heard, ripped open the morning air. The explosion was like thunder overhead, and the birds all over the woods took off with an eerie flutter and then silence. Toby slipped his head up again at field level and saw the rushing back and forth of the Northern soldiers. With quick motions in the trees across the field, the gray hats of the rebels bobbed up and down, showing an incoming burst. A mad scrambling began as the suddenness of a battle startled, shaking everything around the waking troops.

In an instant, a roar went up from the Northerner's' camp. Blue uniforms were dashing forward to another tree line to the left, where Toby could see a group of huge iron guns facing south.

The infantrymen cheered as they assembled in a clearing that Bobby and Toby could see in the woods. Union soldiers mounted horses, columns lined up, and out from the trees came a formation of men that made both boys look at each other shaking. Two hundred yards away from death can make a man or a boy shake like a leaf.

The deadly cannonballs took off through the puffs of white smoke toward the southern part of this once-peaceful peach farm. They promised destruction on land that had known only the fruits of a good man's labor until this September morning. They heard a WOOSH, WOOSH, WOOSH, then, farther away, a THUD, THUD, THUD.

Just then, a rush of movement crunched the ground below them. The boys turned and spied dozens of soldiers in dark blue uniforms whizzing by. They ran quietly, hunched over, carrying long guns with huge gleaming bayonets attached. They gripped clean, new rifles chest-high as they moved— better guns than the Confederates had. Just 20 yards away, up the slope, the men came. The boys ducked down behind some brushes as they realized they had settled right smack dab in the middle of a battle during the Civil War.

BOOM! BOOM! Two shells landed nearby, deafening the woods and tearing up the cabbage field. They could see the shrapnel, the deadly pieces of metal from the bombs, shredding the trees around them. "Keep low, Bobby," Toby whispered, still holding his copy of Uncle Tom's Cabin close to his chest. "We don't want to get kilt before we get a chance to sign up."

There wasn't a chance to run for it now. It was too late. If they moved to go back toward town, they might be mistaken for rebels and shot. "You reckon we should stay here a while 'til they clear out, Toby?" Bobby was trying to say something— anything, so he wouldn't feel that awful fear rising in himself. His throat felt like sandpaper. He wondered how far they were from Antietam Creek and cool water.

"The Rebs are probably set up at the Creek. That's where the bluebellys seem like they wanna go," Toby said. Oh, great, thought Bobby. We're trapped here with no way home and no water. His father ain't gonna get him out of this scrape. "You all right, Bobby?" He must have looked as scared as he really was.

Suddenly the thunder of thousands of rifle shots all going off at once filled the air. The sound felt like suffocation to Bobby. Life was getting sucked out of the whole area, and he could see men in gray falling at the southern tree line. That brave Rebel heart that he wanted to show the Union soldiers in town rapidly faded with every cannonball that landed.

More blue-coated soldiers rushed down the hill below the boys and seemed to be running over the stone bridge that headed toward the Hagerstown Pike.

"They're trying to go around the Rebs and probably tryin' to outflank em' on the east," Toby proclaimed. "There's probably thousands between here and sweet home, so what are we gonna do but sit right here 'til it's over?"

Bobby was thinking how right Toby was again. Only this time he didn't want to hear the facts. It was then he saw the movement in the bushes and the big hand reaching out of the berry patch. As the plant's branches parted, they could see the hand belonged to a Union soldier. Then they saw the blood.

He was wounded, but they couldn't figure out where. There was a dark wet area all over the front of his uniform. "Water!" He mumbled the word as if it were the last one he might say. His eyes were open as he pulled himself over to where his whole body was now visible.

"Help me!"

Bobby looked down at him as if this was one of his own nightmares. The boys looked at each other. They both knew at exactly the same moment that this was no ordinary problem. This was the enemy. Bobby's eyes bulged with amazement.

"Toby, what are we gonna do with a dyin bluebelly?"

Toby looked down at the man who, only a few minutes ago wished was dead and gone. The whole Army of the Potomac should have been dead and gone. He saw the man gasping for air as he lay on his right side. While Bobby stood there dumbfounded,

Toby ripped open his jacket and saw the ugly chest wound. "This man bleedin' to death." He kneeled back away from this ugly surprise and thought. Looking up into the blue and gray clouds, he wondered what his father would do.

"Bobby, see if you can run down that deer trail to the creek. Take my shoe and put the leaves in it like we did last summer. Member? He gonna need some water quick! Ain't nobody gonna shoot you. Most of the troops passed by already."

Bobby did as he was told. He dashed with his head low through an opening in the bush and disappeared. Toby was busy taking off the jacket of the wounded soldier. Toby could see he was an officer. And he could also see that the right side of his chest was where the hole was. He laid him on his back, and the man's eyes closed. The new battlefield medic had to think fast. Then he remembered what his mother had done when she got her leg caught in a fox trap and was alone in the fields. She used a stick for a tourniquet to stop the bleeding.

Toby grabbed the book Uncle Tom's Cabin, the only copy the school had, Bobby said, and placed it over the two-inch wide gash in the officer's chest. He took off the chord he used as a belt and wrapped it tightly around the patient and the book. Finally, he removed his own socks and stuffed them under the chord to make the fit even tighter.

Just as he finished, Bobby returned with the water.

"Seems like the whole army done crossed the creek. The Rebs are on the run, Toby." Bobby saw that his friend had been busy. Somehow he knew that Toby would pick the right thing to do. Should they let a man die in this field, enemy or not, without doing something? He had his answer.

Toby grabbed the shoe that held the priceless liquid, lifted the man's head, and pressed the heel end to his lips. The officer's eyes opened again as the water trickled into his mouth. After shutting his mouth and swallowing the precious water, he looked up at the boys and down at his new appendage. The book was stopping the bleeding now, and his consciousness was returning.

His expression was one of surprise more than pain. Then his eyebrows fell, and he relaxed to the point where he wanted to speak.

"Praise God, and thank you, boys," the man whispered. His chest had to heave toward the sky to push the words out.

Toby and Bobby each grabbed a shoulder and leaned him against a tree. Blood trickled from his mouth.

"Lucky you on the winnin' side today, suh," Toby said.

Bobby stood back and looked at the scene of the black boy who thought he wanted to join the Confederate Army to help protect his homeland, helping an officer of the enemy army. Life was life, he thought.

Maybe when he's old enough to join the army, he'll be shooting at this man, who might be a great general by then, because they saved his life this day. Or maybe the war would end next week, and the more lives saved on either side, the better.

It was near Christmas when Mrs. Morris asked the class if anyone knew anything about this letter she had gotten.

A man from Minnesota wrote a long poetic letter of 'Thank You" to two local boys who used a copy of Uncle Tom's Cabin as a tourniquet on a chest wound and saved his life. The school's address was on the inside cover. They had never told a soul. That would have been aiding the enemy, now, wouldn't it?

1. Why did Bobby bring books home for Toby?
    A. Toby didn't want to go to school.
    B. Toby couldn't go to school because he was black.
    C. So he could eventually keep the books.
    D. He would look good in his mother's eyes.

2. What's the best meaning of conspicuous?
    A. To show off
    B. To be modest
    C. To be easily seen
    D. To be hidden

3. How would you describe Toby?
    A. Mature
    B. Aggressive
    C. Inquisitive
    D. Timorous

4. What is shrapnel?
    A. Pieces of branches that break off.
    B. Parts of an exploded bomb.
    C. Small bullets
    D. Large bombs

5. Why was Bobby's mother most concerned about the boys' reading?

    A. She didn't want to be accused of helping slaves to read.
    B. She didn't want them to steal books.
    C. It would take them away from their chores.
    D. Mrs. Morris would know she was hiding a slave.

6. Since Maryland wasn't a Confederate state, it is all the more surprising that Toby would be _____ to the South.

    A. Hostile
    B. Loyal
    C. Respectful
    D. Generous

7. Why is it ironic that Toby would do what he did? Write a paragraph explaining your answer.

Part Two

Part II illustrates how a U.S. II History class can come alive. Issues arise, and discussions form. From the street urchins of New York at the turn of the century to the homeless hoboes roaming the country during the Depression, we get a close-up of young people from long ago. A long-distance romance during World War II, the protesters of the Vietnam era, and the return of a young warrior from Desert Storm serve to give life to our more recent past.

A City Story

Paper Boys in 1900, New York City

"Shoot!", Runny mumbled. His partially clean white shirt was just the recipient of cherry-colored spit from a combination of Smith Brothers' cough drops and the saliva he was working up after reading the letter he just got from out West. He tried to spooch a good one about five feet out to the curb at the foot of Water Street in New York City. The year was 1898.

Somehow, a combination of fumble lips and venom over the regret of letting Tubby go all the way by himself to Iowa disrupted his aim. The wet wad just landed all over the breast pocket of his shirt. He'd have to wash it tonight anyway, but he still had some venues to visit, and in some of those establishments, he'd be judged by his appearance.

Running numbers in lower Manhattan was ok by Runny. Harmless gaming, it seemed to him. He got to deliver papers in the morning and gambling tickets in the afternoon. Many boys his age were in school and didn't even have one job. He had two. And the latter one was a doozy.

"Guess I'll just button up," Runny said as he swiped away the missed gob. His waist coat was a good one. He tells everyone his mother bought it for him just the week before she died of pneumonia last year. But he actually lifted it off the chair of a sleeping beer drinker at that outside pub area at Hanrahan's on 14th St. Of course, sleeping in it on a stinking mattress didn't help its fragrance.

Why did Tubby have to leave him here in this cold, dirty city? "Buffalo, he says. Who wants to see a stupid Buffalo anyway? Tiny, you ever see a Buffalo?"

"Sure. I seen hunnerts a buffalo. Down at the Rialto Theatre." Tiny, a year younger than Runny and many years behind in savvy, leaned back and took in the big buildings rising around him. "Biggest animal I seen around here is Mrs. O'Leary's wolfhound." He smiled a satisfied smile that showed a small, dark gap where a tooth used to be. "That cowboy Bill Russell shoots plenty. Then he goes on and shoots a couple hunnert Indians."

Runny looked down a couple of inches at the top of Tiny's briar patch of sandy Irish hair and came back with, "Your father's bigger n' that wolfhound. He's more of an animal too."

Ever since Tubby volunteered to live with a family out west, part of the orphan relocation program the City Social Services planned, Runny wondered if he should do the same.

"Must be nice out there, though. Big sky. Lots of grass. And horses to ride."

"Runny, you think Tubby would get on a horse?" Tiny quizzed Runny intently.

"Tiny, I didn't think he'd get on that train, but he did. All the way to gosh darn Ames, Iowa!" This time, he spit a good one landing it right on the sewer cover. "Splat!"

Runny was a gangly lad with smooth, black hair and fiery blue eyes that darted all over the neighborhood. Today, his break between jobs would also consist of detecting the truant officer of his school seeking any stray boys who might be out doing exactly what Tiny and Runny were doing. At 14 years of age in New York City at the turn of the century, the boys thought themselves old enough to earn a living. School was for sissies.

It was a cold February midday, and Tiny still had one newspaper left in his grey canvas bag. He lifted "The New York Journal" out and gazed at the print. "You can't read, Tiny. Who-a you kiddin?" Runny chuckled.

"Maybe not real good, but I can see that this big print here means that some more boys are gonna get buried real soon. Looks like a war comin'. You see what happened down in "Cuber?" Tiny pointed to the newspaper's front page with a huge headline that screamed, 'U.S. WARSHIP SUNK,' and underneath that, 'HUNDREDS KILLED IN EXPLOSION.' I figgered I'd save one these for my grandchildren," meaning the latest copy of the New York Journal. "I ain't seen papers fly out of my hands since the Yankees won the Series last year. Ole Smitty in the barbershop says we're gonna start shootin' Spaniards down there."

"Yeah, war sure is good for selling newspapers. That sour puss, Mr. Hearst, could make a lot more money if we sent a bunch of boys down there. Just think, would you rather read about a couple a more people dying of TB around here or our guys blowin' the heck out of the Spanish tin cans in Cuba? You know how close that is to Florida?" Runny usually one-upped his little partner, and this was no exception.

"Runny, you think we could sign up?" A light bulb lit up in Tiny's head. "Goin' down there and shootin' Spaniards beats the heck outta seein' stupid buffaloes in Ohio!"

"Iowa, ya nincompoop! And anyway, I'm not chasing Tubby all around the country. Hats off to him. Maybe he'll come back rich. We're doin' plenty good right here in the city."

Runny seemed to be thinking about a hundred things at once. He bent his lean neck back to look at two Italian workers in tattered, thick shirts across the street, shivering while they slid mason trowels over the bricks of a brand-new apartment house. They were on a wobbly platform with a bucket, and every few minutes, they would look down at the sidewalk three stories beneath their feet. It was February in the city.

The newsboys wondered how much the Italians were paid for that dangerous work. How fortunate they were for being able to make the money they did. How else could a kid who ignores the obligation of school ever make it in this city? The numbers running in the afternoon brought them into contact with a type of person no school boy would normally meet. But nobody's interfered with their enterprise yet.

Of course, no one supervised their daily rounds in either boy's case. Runny's parents died before he was 13, and Tiny's mom just left the family last month. He never knew his father. They were too typical of the thousands of street urchins who filled the great Eastern cities.

The shabbily built tenements welcomed immigrants by the boat load. Cheap-looking structures would shoot up to the sky in a matter of days. No sooner would the roof be tar papered than 20 families from Hungary, Poland, or Sweden would bring their rucksacks and newly born babies and plant themselves inside.

Runny could turn his gaze to the south from the top of his building, looking over the harbor of New York. There, one could survey the forest of masts that seemed stuck into the water like one huge sea urchin. The commercial fleet of ships that filled every inch of navigable waters around the island was the lifeblood of the city.

Nothing moves in New York unless the big sailing vessels first get it from abroad. Not too long ago, one of those big square riggers brought Runny's small family here from Ireland. But now, like so many other young people, he was on his own. How, he sometimes thought, could a kid less skillful make a go of it here? He was blessed with a gift of blarney and could talk his way into quite a few jobs he'd never done. The boss usually liked his resourcefulness.

Not like Billy Shea. Poor Billy tried to run a few messages around Wall Street, making some quick cash but he never made it back to his mother's tiny room in the 1200 block of 15th St. He was found with his hands tied behind his back, attached to ropes that bound his legs underneath him. He had a mouthful of crumpled papers with small numbers handwritten on them. The police also said this was not the first time they found a youngster like Billy "deader than a flounder," shot in the back of the head for the small number of bills someone could grab from him. He was in an alley, one stench-filled block from where Runny laid his head last night.

T.R. himself investigated the murder of Billy Shea. Roosevelt was a police commissioner at the time and embodied a man who got things done. But they never found the one who shot "Sweet William." Only five kids showed up when the local social workers put him in the ground at Potter's Field. Teddy Roosevelt had bigger things to think about at the time.

"Maybe old Teddy Roosevelt wants to be President or something. Says here he wants America to be ready for war. What the heck did we do to get a rise out of the Spanish anyway, Runny?" Tiny was moving his finger over the print of The Journal as he leaned against the lamppost at the corner of Cherry St.

These two products of the teeming tenements saw the unstemmed flow of people off those boats just a few blocks away. How many of them could speak English? How many brought only a knapsack? How many brought the dreaded virus that killed so many in cities from Baltimore to Boston? The cities became choked with people from other continents, and soon the quality of life would suffer to the point of breaking.

You didn't have to read The Journal to know about the constant fires that consumed buildings daily in lower Manhattan. Without the luxury of natural gas or electricity, coal was the heating fuel of the time. Many of these quickly built immigrant rooming houses didn't even contain pipes to carry the heat to all the rooms. Some newcomers found the toilets didn't work, especially on the top floors, which was unfortunate.

The streets were crowded with combinations of transportation. Horses were the workers of the brick-covered streets. There were also trolley cars with electric connections overhead that posed a danger for curious children who might want to climb out their window to touch the wires. Of course, one finger on it and Zap!

A few motorcars had arrived on the New York scene with big leather seats, heavy metal bumpers, and wooden spokes inside rubber tubes for wheels.

They usually scared the horses pulling the carts. The one approaching the boys on Water St and Cherry had no carriage. It was like a square, black, metal box with one man in the front with a long white raincoat and a pair of goggles on. Behind him in the passenger seat were two men, one of whom threw down a half-smoked cigar as the car screeched up to the curb.

"Hey, Runny. Get over here!" He was a fat, balding man with an expensive English-tailored suit. His partner was a younger, thin, freckled gentleman who was as quiet as a mannequin. "You little louse, come here!" The fat man's face reddened. Runny thought it could be the whiskey. Mr. Winckom always had lunch at Hanrahan's. Tiny jumped back away from the iron lamp post as Runny hesitantly stepped forward.

"What is it, Mr. Winckom? Everyone get the right numbers yesterday?" Runny asked nervously. He remembered when Bobby Collins ran for Winckom down in Wall Street and dripped some hot chocolate on some papers. By the time the bets got to the "Charlie Gang," they were indecipherable. He tried to cover over the mess with his own handwriting, but the numbers turned out all wrong. The players never got the money for the number they backed. Bobby got beaten pretty badly before he skedaddled to New Jersey for good.

"Runny," Winckom said, "I want to move you up in the world. You've been running around here like a little ragamuffin long enough. I want you to do me a favor. Maybe if it goes well, we could move you into a room in the building next to mine. How does that sound?"

"What do I have to do?" Runny thought about the tenement next to the apartment house that Mr. Winckom owned. It wasn't much better than the unheated cellar he and a couple of boys shared off his alley.

Winckom got out of the car, reached out, and pulled Runny's coat. "Start a little fire, is all. These Jews over on Mott Street are starting an organization I don't like, and it's time my insurance company went to work. Now there won't be any risk to you, me boy'o. Just do as I say, and nobody has a problem."

Runny's thoughts raced ahead of the moment, and he thought of his own room with a coal-burning stove and window to look over the harbor at South St., and a brand new bicycle and...

"But Mr. Winckom, I can't do anything like that. What if one of those folks gets burned up? Just like the O'Malleys over on 3rd St.?" He shivered when he thought of the tenement that collapsed on the two little kids and their dog.

Winckom turned to his partner, still in the car, and glared back at Runny. "There's so many fires started by these ignorant....nobody's gonna find out. What do you care about those people anyway?" He thought one last time, narrowed his eyes, and brought his whiskey-smelling snout within inches of Runny's. "And if ya don't, I'll have that truant officer O'Toole on your backside so fast you won't be able to say, 'Jack be nimble.' You'd be back in school, learnin' the golden rule, and not making any gold at all out here on the streets."

The fat man squeezed into the back seat as the driver in the white raincoat opened the door for him. Runny got no closer. Winckom gathered himself and said, "You give me an answer today. I'll be back here at 4 o'clock. You be here too." The driver went to the front of the car with a cranking rod in his hand, inserted it into an opening, and wound the engine up a couple of times. It coughed once, started with a rumble, and slid off into the noisy, mixed traffic of New York City.

"You hear that, Tiny? He wants me to fire up a place to get the Jew organizers out. How the heck does he think I got THAT in me?" Runny looked unbelieving. His eyebrows were arched, and his face squeezed tight with the biggest challenge of his young life laid out flat before him.

As Tiny scurried over to Runny, they slowly edged up against the wall of the butcher shop. "Maybe he thinks you got no choice. Your mother's gone, your father's gone, and it's Godawful cold these days. And that cellar ain't no warmer." Tiny was sympathetic to his friend's dilemma but glad too. He hadn't been approached by any gang leader to do somebody's nasty work. "And if O'Toole gets you this time, you'll be in jail for a week before they let you back into school."

"Why is he afraid of making those buildings right? They have no ventilation. There's no light. They're lucky if they have water. Those poor people right off the boats are dyin' like flies. And all because Winckom doesn't think they'll complain. Boxed in like sardines, they have no choice. Where are they gonna go, Tiny?"

"What are ya gonna do, Runny?"

At the moment, he just didn't know. There were remnants of snow on the ground, and the skies were grey. It's probably going to snow again tonight, Runny thought. If he decided not to do Winckom's bidding, he would have to be the one to figure out where to go. The fat man would not want witnesses to discuss his evil intentions. Runny thought back to poor Billy. Found like that. Flat out cold with a bullet in his head. That could be him!

In New York City in 1898, the crush of immigrants from Europe was becoming a huge problem. People of different backgrounds and languages trying to make a new start in a foreign city led to confusion that was hard to unravel. The authorities were behind in their policing because of these masses of people. If the police didn't understand a foreign language, justice for the newcomers might not happen.

Crime against immigrants soared. It was easy for criminals to exploit those who couldn't speak English yet. Robbery and murder were at an all-time high in the city. And so was the natural death rate. Many died because of the poor housing they endured at the hands of men like Winckom. And many orphans roamed the streets.

They could live at the Paupers Barracks or the Children's Aid Society or with distant relatives who found it hard to feed another mouth. Some kids had to make a living any way they knew how like the newsboys and the bootblacks who would do almost anything for a handful of nickels.

Later that cold February evening, Tiny gave up looking for Runny. Someone said he went to his "thinking place" to figure out the situation. He didn't think Runny was the kind of guy who would burn down somebody's building and maybe kill someone. But what choice does a kid have? The Fat Man would find him sooner or later, and by that time, the troublemakers' house would be burned down by some other street boy.

He wasn't at the water tower. He wasn't in the barbershop. Heck! Runny only saved 50 bucks after bailing out other newsboys from tight spots like this. Where could he be? Tiny finally went down to the cellar where they stayed, and on the mattress where Runny would sleep in the chilly winter nights with his frayed but thick waistcoat around him, there was a piece of white paper. It read, "Tell the Fat Man to go to hell! I'm off to see the Buffalo."

In a few weeks, fresh from the headlines of the Maine's sinking, Teddy Roosevelt would recruit Rough Riders to march through Cuba and eventually up San Juan Hill. The two street boys could have used T.R. to help solve the problem. At the very least, he might chase down a tenement builder like Winckom, but that was wishful thinking. The Commissioner would give him a good poke in the eye before he locked him up, but he was not to be found. Neither was a tough little kid named Runny, just one more lost boy from the City of New York.

Discussion Questions

1. What do you know about Ellis Island?

2. What do you think the people in the tenements could do after they organized themselves?

3. Why do you think there were so many orphans at the turn of the century?

4. Why would some politicians be more concerned with the upcoming Spanish-American War than the problems of the cities?

Up The Creek

Barrels of Whiskey During the 1920's

My grandfather used to sit around the table on Saturday mornings, telling my friends from the neighborhood and me tales of his youth. Some would be about pick-up baseball games with exaggerated descriptions of dramatic moments. Others would revolve around how someone got a nickname that stuck throughout World War I. But one I particularly enjoyed was the one about the rum runners of Cheesequake Creek.

During the 1920's alcohol was made illegal, and nobody liked that very much around the small coastal towns of New

Jersey, especially in the summer when the folks from the big cities would cruise down in their noisy cars to cool off. Big black Pearce-Arrows, model T's, and even a Duesenberg or two could be seen flying down Rt. 35 on the way to Asbury Park or Long Branch.

These Jersey shore towns provided amusement for the "swells" from up North, my grandfather would say. The big cars would be stuffed with people, baggage, and beach balls. But a diversion on the three-hour drive home would be welcome for those who had to drive back the same day to Newark, Jersey City, or Patterson. On a Friday or Saturday night, it would actually be the main destination of the city folks. First, the bumpy ride down to the beach in any jalopy you could manage, fry like fish on the smoldering sand, eat some flounder somewhere near Keyport, and head to Morgan on the bluffs of the inlet to dance.

I said, "Pop Pop. There's no place to dance around here now." My friends would giggle. They were just at the stage where they found that Vitalis helped their hair to slick back, and the girls found that cool. They wondered what "cool" was in the 1920s.

"In those days," Pop Pop continued with an amused twinkle in his eye, "there were quite a few places that were really hoppin."

"How come?"

"Simple. Prohibition."

And he proceeded to explain the changes that took place because the government wanted to try what he said was an experiment. No alcohol was allowed to be made or sold anywhere in the United States. It didn't take long for the public to react negatively to this unusual law. My grandfather said that they took away one of the pleasures of life. Next, they would take away cigarettes as he puffed on a non-filter Camel at the breakfast table.

Ambitious folks would make their own beer. Heck! Aunty Betty was making gin in her bathtub for her card-party friends down at Morgan Creek. A few old cabins expanded and served fried fish and coleslaw. Even Millie's Bait Shop started serving food. But the real attraction was liquor: rum from Cuba, whiskey from Canada, and beer from, well, right up the street. And on the weekends there would be bands and dancing.

One night, there was a problem getting the contraband into the dance halls. The usual ships that brought the stuff into the Raritan Bay were held up near Philadelphia. Some said the Feds took their whole cargo. The FBI was on the tail of any illegal shipments, bootlegging as it was called then.

Since it was a Friday afternoon, the wooden shack "restaurant" owners were getting a little nervous. There was no sign of Shorty, Stosh, or any other boat owner who would usually speed out into the Bay and even past Sandy Hook into the ocean off New York to meet the big boats. They would steam in from the Caribbean, having dropped off their crates of rum at Baltimore, then Philadelphia, and then New York city. Sometimes, with a good pair of spyglasses, as my grandfather called them, you could see Canadian markings on the steamer. But this particular Friday none of the speed boats that would dash out to meet them were heard from. These boats had no phones.

The trucks that waited a mile or so up the creek had been there since early that morning. By now, the Luhrs skiffs with the huge inboard engines would have made their way up the shallow maze of waterways. The tall reeds on either side of the creek would hide their route if any authorities cared to follow them. The Coast Guard vessels occasionally pulled one of the skiffs over to search the open bay but could not reach the creek's headwaters where it was too shallow.

Theirs was a heavy 40-foot ship. Once they passed through the open railroad bridge, the water became dangerously low, and the Coastguard boat could run aground. The bottom would extend ten feet down into the dark water sticking into the mud. When the truckers saw the chase boat give up in the darkness and turn back toward the inlet, they would laugh and lay their hands on the horn. The searchlight would be extinguished, and those ashore could see the red lights of the stern. Shorty and Stosh would unload, and the wooden shack restaurants and other establishments throughout the county were in business. This was the Roaring 20's.

Mrs. Donovan and Bobby Pulaski leaned over the rail of the marina gangplank as they anxiously peered up the inlet toward the bay.

"Bobby, I hope nothin' happened to those two. Never mind the business tonight. What if they hit the sandbar out there and flipped? I'd never forgive myself," she said. She rubbed her hands as if washing off grease.

"Naw. There's two boats, the best watermen on the bay, and a big stack of dollars waitin' here for 'em. They'll show." Pulaski sounded as if he was trying to convince himself. It was a hot August day. The whole Jersey Shore was packed from Sandy Hook to Atlantic City, and a large migration back north was only a couple of hours away. "What if I got no hootch to serve those swells from Bayonne? I'd be better off closed. Tell 'em we all got summer pneumonia."

Just then, the low drone of engines drifted across the still bay. In a few seconds, the hot sticky air carried a louder hum like a trombone stuck on one note, and then the slap-slap-slap as the boat hulls hit the water. The two club owners dashed down to the dock to see the two wooden skiffs barreling down the inlet with the rock jetties on either side framing a welcome sight.

From their perspective, the only way to see the end of the inlet was if the train bridge were open. Otherwise, most of the vision of the bay and beyond was blocked. The large section of two sets of tracks would be held flat down most of the time when the Jersey Central train would regularly pass by on the way to New York north or all the way to Point Pleasant headed south. The bridge tender would then winch it up for any boat needing headroom to pass through.

Today the tide was high in the creek, and passing under the bridge in the closed position was impossible. So as a growing number of locals lined up on nearby Morgan Hill, Shorty and Stosh waived to the bridge tender who graciously raised the monstrosity. Stosh's brother waved back with a fistful of dollars in his hand. The men slowed the engines of the two boats and quietly turned up the meandering, snaking waterway. Just before Shorty's skiff rounded out of sight, he lofted a case with his two beefy arms chest-high for the growing number of spectators on the hill to see. The bridge was lowered flat again and Morgan nightlife was back in business.

If Babe Ruth had hit a home run right before their eyes, it wouldn't have been more of a thrill, especially when they saw what was coming through the inlet now. It was a huge Coast Guard cruiser—three white-uniformed sailors, two with rifles raised, pointing straight ahead to guide the driver. The cruiser's engine sounded like an airplane taking off as it roared down the inlet.

A huge wake washed up on the rock jetty and washed bait boxes away from a couple of fishermen. But just as it made the halfway point of its entry and slowed to a more civilized speed, the sailors on the bow of the decelerating boat realized something was amiss. The bridge was down. As a final wave washed from the propeller of the Coast Guard cruiser toward the shore, it stopped like a speeding horse being reined in. Through a quickly hoisted megaphone, the captain at the wheel yelled up to Lenny, "Open that bridge!"

The silence that followed drew the attention of every resident of the small cabins and bungalows from the Hill. Fishermen cleaning their fish on the docks looked to the government boat waiting for Lenny's response. Even little children stopped their backyard games to see what was happening.

Lenny called out from the little shed on the Morgan side of the bridge, "It won't open, Cap'n. It's stuck down. The grease ran dry. Gotta get some grease for the cables." With that, barrel-bellied Lenny waddled out of the shed and began to walk up the trestled tracks to make a bid for repairs. "I'll be right back, Cap'n. Boatworks right down there got some grease."

The eruption of laughter from the docks echoed up to the hill and all through the line of spectators who saw the dilemma of the sailors. They might have made it up the creek with a higher tide if the bridge was open to intercept the bootleggers. But once again, they were turned away. The bridge wouldn't move. The captain picked up his megaphone once more. "We'll return tomorrow, sir," he barked to Lenny. "And this time with an inspection team. You'll be off that bridge and back digging clams!"

Lenny turned around, cupped his hand to his ear, and yelled," Clams Cap'n? You want clams — go on up to Fritzy's. They got great steamed clams tonight." And he kept on walking. The locals howled and hooted. The captain turned his angry gaze toward the fishermen and glanced up the hill. This was hard work, this Prohibition. He turned the cruiser around in a tight circle and headed out to the bay with a wake that rocked every boat in the creek. It looked as though even the small rowboats were howling.

*****

My grandfather looked down at the boys at the breakfast table and smiled. "They didn't much care for the Feds in those days. Even if you weren't a drinker — it seems like they got a little too close to takin' away peoples' rights. And my cousin George didn't even like police for years after."

"How come, Pop Pop?"

He blew a big cloud of blue smoke over the kitchen from his non-filter Camel. "Cause that night, his girlfriend and he went dancing at Fritzy's, and some darn state trooper in plain clothes stole her away. Never saw her since."

"Well, what was the trooper doin' in a place that sold illegal stuff?" I asked.

Pop Pop blew another puff of smoke and smiled a big wide grin.

"Shucks," he said, "the local cops had to wait until the mayor left before they could go in. But they were there every night." He leaned forward as if the moral of the story was coming. But he only ended the tale with, "That's why George didn't trust anybody in uniform until Pearl Harbor."

Discussion Questions

1. What is the setting for the story?

2. Who are the "swells"?

3. Whose side of the prohibition question were the local
   residents on? Why?

4. What were some reasons the Prohibition law would be
   repealed?

Hobo

Breadlines for the Poor

After the stock market disaster of 1929 and the dust bowl droughts of the Midwest, there began roaming an American gypsy known as the hobo. There wasn't just one. There were thousands. There were thousands of thousands.

Whole families packed up what was left of their lives and traveled in search of work. They went to California to pick fruit. They moved to Chicago to pack meat. They moved to New York to work in a clothing factory. If they could get work, they sent word back to Kansas, Oklahoma, and Missouri, and wherever they were from that, even if it were only for a couple of weeks, food was being put on the table.

Sometimes it was too risky to ask your whole family to leave the place they were born and travel to unknown destinations, so single men began to wander the land. The hoboes were becoming part of the American scene. They were grim evidence that the economic system that ruled this country wasn't working. Something had to change soon.

Bill Patrick was a hobo. He didn't think of himself as such. But when the factory shut down in his small town in Ohio, he left everyone he had ever known and jumped on a freight car heading west. Bill didn't know where he found himself the next day, only that his canteen of water was empty and his stomach was rumbling.

It turned out that his unplanned destination was as small a town as he had just left. Plopping to the ground, he could see a large enough building to be a factory just a few yards from the train yard in the morning air. His optimism turned sour when he saw a few more bums leap from the freight train two cars ahead.

"Hey, there's a couple hoboes just jumped out up there!" He could hear yelling and began to run around the small sheds surrounding the train yard. The police must have the place staked out. He saw the other two men climb up a ladder to disappear onto a roof. These were not good times.

Wandering away from the chase, Bill forgot about the building, which stood silent, closed. Ambling down a dusty road from the tiny town, he wondered where he could be safe. Second, how would he eat tonight? After a mile or so, he hesitated after seeing an "X" on the curb in front of a three-story house. Remembering a story a homeless friend from Ohio told, he wanted to find out if it were true. Did the hoboes really mark the houses where people would feed the needy? Did he ever think when he first heard the story that he would get to know about the mark firsthand?

Suddenly a door opened. "Hungry? Come on in here." A matronly woman with an apron around a portly belly seemed like a light in the darkness of Bill's life. She smiled as if she knew him. She did know his kind. These were not just drifters giving up on life and looking for a handout. These were American survivors of a nationwide disaster. Bill felt welcome, and he climbed the stairs of the porch and walked into the house behind the waddling woman.

Introductions were made around a table of middle-aged men, a half dozen ill-clad wanderers. Graciously he sat down to baked chicken and biscuits. Mrs. Walling was her name, and she always made a little extra food every time she cooked, what with this being a railroad town in Iowa. The corn belt farmers were being hit hard, just like everywhere else. Men were looking for work all over. And she could understand why so many were walking around, hitching rides, and jumping freights.

Police had no right to chase these otherwise good Americans from their natural instincts to make a living. She set aside plates, forks, and knives for the "visitors." Her husband, Mr. Walling, who worked in city hall, never minded her taking in guests, even if they left only pennies for their meals. The local government would be the last thing the Depression would affect. Factory workers weren't so lucky. There used to be 20,000 people in this town. The Depression took their jobs. Then the banks took their homes. Mrs. Walling had seen many of them just take their clothes and move in with relatives who still had jobs. Sometimes they had to move out of state. She said, "The man who owned the feed store had to close last month. He took his three children and moved to Chicago. The last thing he said was, 'At least they got soup lines there.' Can you imagine, Mr. Patrick?" Bill Patrick knew what she meant.

On the mantel was a picture of Franklin Roosevelt, smiling, eyes twinkling. He looked on with warm recognition of the Walling residence in Ames, Iowa. Mrs. Walling turned away as the men gorged themselves at the table. From the sink, she continued, "My son, Jerry, will be home tomorrow. He manages a canning factory in Des Moines. Maybe he's got work over there, Mr. Patrick."

"Well, I thought I'd take a look around here and see if they're hiring," Bill said. There had to be some seed and feed stores, tanneries, or maybe a mechanic that could use someone.

A burly man with a huge mustache burst out a warning, "Ain't no work around here, boy. We been looking all week."

"Well, I've got to do my own roamin' tomorrow morning and see what's what." After his delightful dinner, Bill got up slowly and gave a half-smile to Mrs. Walling.

"Now, my husband'll be home in a few minutes. Would you like to stay for a little dessert?" She had a pleading look to her that was well-practiced. It was a show of understanding that Bill could appreciate. But he knew not to overstay his welcome. He shook his head.

"Mr. Patrick, you come back about the same time tomorrow night, and my son Jay will be home from Des Moines. He's got a great job at the cannery. If he can't get you anything in Des Moines, maybe he knows of a job outside the city. By that time, I'll have talked to my husband too."

Bill winced with a painful, twisted expression on his face. He knew right then there were no jobs in Ames, Iowa. "Thanks, Mrs. Walling. Maybe I'll do just that!" He shook her hand warmly, picked up his small canvas bag, and waved to the remaining men, who just grunted a salute. He walked down the stairs into a chilly, autumn, Midwestern evening.

After a night in a farmer's tool shed and rambling the whole next day, Bill had talked to plenty of people. None of them had an optimistic disposition. Even though the sunny skies ruled the weather patterns, they didn't lighten the gloom of the local populace. Bill spent his last dime on a cup of coffee and a muffin late that afternoon. He reheard Mrs. Walling's words about dinner and her son. He looked like quite a professional man in the picture next to President Roosevelt. Probably graduated from the University of Iowa. He had a big car and a fine house on a lake. Some guys could just slice right through this Depression. Bill recalled a picture of his own family. Showing his fine haircut in a dark Sunday suit, he stood beside his parents on their porch. What would the Patricks' say to the Wallings if they met?

No work today. After walking to every place of business he could, Bill realized that Ames was in trouble too. The local paper had very few job listings unless you wanted to sell pots and pans door to door. The headlines echoed the times: Ford Laying Off Workers in Detroit, Breadlines in St. Louis, Employees at Factory Take Pay Cut.

Bill thought how grand it would be to have that Walling kid's job. He'd be out at the lake right now, away from the panhandlers and bums, just dropping a line into a seamless, quiet stream. And maybe even catch a fish! But life was turning out differently for him. A momentary dream.

On the afternoon of the second day, a Saturday, he could hear the familiar roars from a radio coming from a small cottage. The University of Iowa - Notre Dame football game blared out loud. Thousands were screaming for a touchdown, but he just wanted a sandwich.

"I wasn't brought up to be a freeloader," he thought. Yet nothing at all to eat today was making him weak. This day he had tried all the nearby farms. Very few had phones. He didn't have the money to call them anyway, so he had to walk miles to knock on a door.

He held his head high as if he were a nobleman—not a hobo, a traveling bum. Of course, he would work, but it was never offered. Many fields had gone to dust. The farmers were now forced to sell the last of their livestock to make it through the winter. The cheers of the football game sounded like mocking laughter as he walked toward the railroad yard. A stadium full of people having the time of their lives while the other half of America was worried or hungry.

Then, he made a decisive turn toward the Wallings.

" Just one more meal before I head out of town," Bill said. "They are such caring people." To see that hopeful smile would do him a world of good before he turned back to the uncertainty of freight cars. But a strange scene unfolded as the big white house came into view. A doctor was stepping into a big black car, dressed in his long white hospital garb, waving goodbye to a sobbing Mrs. Walling as her husband walked back into the house.

Bill was standing right over the little painted "X" on the curbside as he looked around, wondering if he should climb the stairs to the house or stay away. Their son should be home by now. He could probably take care of things. He looked like a man who could take care of things. But Bill's shoulders sagged when he overheard two neighbors talking near him.

It turned out that Jerry Walling, the Gold n' Greens plant manager in Des Moines, Iowa, had hit a bit of bad luck himself.

The cannery had been closed a month ago, and Jerry didn't have the heart to let his parents know. There was too much pride at stake. He thought the owners were not telling the truth when they said the business would be reopened soon.

Bill leaned into the conversation a little more and heard that Jerry finally came home today, his birthday, by way of a box car on the Illinois Central. Bearded and weak, he fell off the train. The Ames police were waiting. They didn't believe him when he said he was Jerry Walling, so they took the poor man to the house to prove who he was. Mrs. Walling fainted. Mr. Walling broke down in tears. Jerry kept staring ahead. The neighbors had all already seen an uncertain future for their families and friends. They knew what it felt like. Americans in the 1920s were trying to find their way out of dark days.

Just moments ago, before Bill got to the house, young Jerry fell to the sidewalk, seized with sadness his parents took for a nervous breakdown.

He whispered to them, "I'm sorry. Sorry for the trouble."

They called Dr. Swenson. But the clean-cut man with the stylish suit and the unlimited possibilities, with the home on the lake and the elegant girlfriend, with the country club membership and season tickets to Iowa football games, just went bust in the big city. It was 1936, in the middle of the biggest Depression to ever hit this country. No one was immune. The doctor was on the way, but not much use.

Bill Patrick climbed on board the next freight at about midnight to take him back to Ohio. Somehow he knew everything would happen if he stood in one place long enough. That place would be where he had friends and relatives who could help each other until this miserable time for the working man would end. One day a wage earner — the next day a hobo. These were the worst of times.

Discussion Questions

1. Why did the police chase the hoboes?

2. What did Americans think about the Great Depression?

3. Why did Jerry Walling come home by a freight train?

4. Writing prompt: Write a letter home as Bill Patrick.

A Movie to Remember

The Welcome Home Kiss. San Diego Statue

George Mitchell remembered standing in line at the Grauman Theatre in Hollywood with his intended, Miss Daisy Williams. She was telling him about this fantastic picture she had seen at the Lido last Sunday, *Citizen Kane*.

"Orson Welles is such a great actor," she said. "I thought I was right there with him."

"But now you're right here with me, where you belong. And we're going to see a heck of a movie tonight. Did you ever hear about Sergeant York and how he captured all those Germans single-handed?" George recalled looking into her eyes on the boulevard in Hollywood while the world seemed like a dream.

Even though the war was erupting in Europe, he had college to go through. UCLA was only a few months away. He and Daisy would both reap the benefits of his taking a business degree. When they were in front of her parents, she would always ask how his father's dry cleaning business was doing over on Sunset Ave. George proudly said he'd like to expand and build a few more.

But that warm and scented evening in front of the famous Chinese Theatre of Hollywood had an ominous side. As they left arm in arm, George stopped to get a newspaper at the sidewalk stand. The date in the upper left-hand corner read:

"December 6, 1941."

"Private, dig that hole deeper, or Tojo himself is gonna make a poster boy of you. It'll say, 'Welcome, G.I.s to the Philippines. Thank you for standing up for your country.' You get your bag of bones farther down toward New York City with that entrenching tool, or I'll pound on top of that brand new helmet until your spittin' subway nickels!"

George was shocked back into the real world by Sergeant Fabini. Here they were, in the Borrego Valley Badlands, a desert, training for jungle-warfare. The new recruits who had just arrived in training camp would get the usual treatment until some real action came their way. All the new guys knew this. But did he have to interrupt such a dream? Beautiful Daisy under the soft lights of a world-famous theatre. Home and all the promises that went with it, were tossed aside by Sgt.

Fabini. The thought of a jungle was frightening enough without the obnoxious man with the stripes on his arm in charge of George's very life. And would he ever get rid of that stupid unlit cigar?

Daisy was getting ready for work just a couple of hundred miles yet a world away . It seemed that George had been gone for years now. It had only been a couple of months. The new job at the phone company was fine, but life was so lonely without him, without plans, without a future. He had enlisted after their night at the movies in Hollywood and signed up for four years in the army. Although there was enough reason to stop the war that started that December 7th, George would return before those four years if the war ended sooner.

As Daisy reached the bus for downtown Los Angeles, she questioned when her real life would start. She had spent the most wonderful moments with this sandy-haired boy, and then he was gone; it was like leaving the movie theatre before the story finished. She took a seat on the noisy bus and thought about where his next move would be after he left training camp. *I wonder what he's doing at this very moment.*

At 8:15 A.M. in training camp, he was practicing with his heavy rifle in ambush drills and entrenching tools. He couldn't wait until he got to his combat post. *If only I had a lighter M-1 rifle to carry.*

"Hey, George. This ain't so bad. I heard over in Oklahoma they're training with sticks. There aren't enough guns to go around." His pal Donny Sylvester was a San Diego lifeguard and in a little better shape than George. The morning exercise was firming him up, but he knew there would be no time for practice when they got closer to the action. And there might not be time to think of Daisy as he was every hour here. Whether it was on the parade grounds grinding through drill and ceremony, in the middle of the gas room with his mask off repeating his service number, or lining up inside the dummy landing craft, he would see her face and wonder what she was doing at that moment.

That Friday afternoon, Daisy was on her way home to her parents. She recently got a promotion at the telephone company but couldn't afford a car, so she found herself on the same old bus. *Even if I were the manager of the whole operator staff, I couldn't get enough gas to make driving a regular habit.* She didn't have a gas ration booklet. She wondered if there would be enough gas for the family to go to Will Rogers State Beach that weekend.

"Drive To Victory!" the billboards downtown read, "Not for fun!"

Los Angeles was spreading out, and the only way to get anywhere outside of town was by car. Yet the gallons of gas it took to drive them were precious. There were long lines at gas stations when there was gas to be sold. Sitting on the bus ride home, she wondered if George was using some of the gas meant for the military on his new assignment. *Where is he now?*

*****

George and Donny got to stay together, and on the huge troop ship that sliced through the South Pacific, the soldiers asked many questions. There were few answers.

"Donny, you ever heard of the Marshall Islands before? That's where they say we're headed."

"Must be Admiral Nimitz has a vacation home there. I hear it's loaded with beautiful palm trees and nice white beaches. And island girls can't wait to meet us." Donny always found a way to make light of a situation. Someone had to crack a few jokes as the dark clouds hovered above the troop ship. The voyage was not going well with huge storms. Soldiers not used to the steady rolling through ocean waves became sick. Days of staying in the tiny bunks attached to the inside of the hull was no way to fight a war.

George leaned over to Donny, who was playing solitaire on the bottom bunk, "You mean it's a welcoming committee with snipers and Japs in caves. Just what we need."

The sailors would laugh at the "grunts" doing the mop-up duties after the Marines hit the beach. It was called "island hopping."

After the Marshalls, there would be the Marianas, then back to the Philippines, where MacArthur was defeated. And finally, they hoped to walk into Tokyo and relieve the Emperor of his throne. Until then, it was misery on this tin can at sea. George wrote his letter to Daisy and tried to picture what she would be doing now.

Daisy received the letter Friday at 5:15 P.M.
"Look, Mother. They're tearing out holes in the letters again," Daisy cried out.

Military Intelligence poured over every letter, taking out messages that showed locations or troop movements.

Daisy tore open the envelope, and her mother tried to read along over her shoulder.

"Where is he now?" her mother asked. "I do hope he doesn't have to go through any terrible invasion.

"I hope that doesn't mean he's in a hell-hole jungle waiting to get shot at," Daisy said.

"Daisy Williams, that's no way to talk." Her mother retreated to her big stuffed chair in the sitting room. "I'm sure he'll come home in one piece. But I can't see anyone standing that kind of duty. Mosquitos and malaria and Japanese with bayonets. Oh, I just can't think about it." Her mother picked up the evening newspaper, but it was slammed back down onto the coffee table almost as soon as she did. "I'll go fix supper."

Somebody has to go on as if life were normal, and that would be Mother. Daisy was too worried about her soldier across the sea. There should only be one 'Rosy the Riveter' worrying about one G.I. Joe at a time.

*****

"The leg will be fine, Sergeant Dill. I'll be reporting for duty tomorrow. I don't like Hawaii this time of year anyway." George sat up in his cot somewhere on an island called Okinawa and worried about getting meat for dinner. A good enough leg wound would have gotten him to a Hawaii hospital. Shrapnel from a booby trap only ripped through his calf muscle, missing bone by a tiny bit. At least those who were in the field tent would get meat. Those with all their body parts intact got the same old canned c- rations. The war was not over for him yet. He wondered if he should even write Daisy that he was wounded.

*****

It was sad for Daisy at the U.S.O. club in Los Angeles, but her two friends were dancing up a storm as the band played Glen Miller tunes. They would swing, sway, and even dance the slow songs with boys who might be shipping out the next day for war zones unknown. She would sit and smile and think about George. These young men could go home to their wives and girlfriends when this was over. They were getting good at pretending.

*****

George and Donny were reading the military paper and how the Marines took Iwo Jima. It was Sunday morning, and they were tired of digging in. "Those Japs are long gone, my friend, and they still have us filling sandbags. Why don't they get us a new jungle or fly us back to California, U.S.A.?" George asked his buddy.

Donny smiled and said, "Are you kidding? They'll have us going through this island with a fly swatter, doing our part to rid the world of disease before they fly us home. With the pay we're getting, they expect results." He turned back to his paper, and George did the same.

*****

Daisy had already read the news of the Allied victory in the Los Angeles Times on the front porch. She'd be getting ready for dinner about now, and George thought about how she might hear on the radio that the invasion of Japan was next. How he hoped she would not be afraid for him.

President Truman came on the radio at 6 P.M. that Sunday evening and congratulated the Allied forces for carrying the war all the way to the Emperor's front door. General MacArthur was heard to be begging to be the general to lead the invasion. George wondered how many would die this time. Then the news came. The world shook with word of the atomic bomb at Hiroshima.

*****

"George, it's all over. Did ya hear. Did ya hear about them dropping the big one?" Donny ran into the barracks in his usual sweat-soaked fatigues. "Let's see 'em come back from this one!" Two days later, it did take another one. With the Emperor of Japan silent, the city of Nagasaki was hit too. The official word came to Okinawa and throughout the Pacific. This world war had ended. Canadian soldiers, the French, Spanish, Filipino, Chinese, and even Indian troops were going home. The California boys were too.

*****

"Make sure you save those meat stamps, Mother," Daisy said. "I sure would love to cook his first meal at home. It says here troop ships are arriving every day from all over. I haven't gotten a letter since last week before they bombed Japan, but he must be arriving this week." Daisy was breathless when the news was announced. "Mother, at least don't use up all the gas. We should call the Mitchells and offer to drive them to San Diego when we find out about the ship."

Mrs. Williams stood with a confident pose in the parlor and said, "He should be cabling us from the ship. I went through this with your uncle back in the First World War. Only he was coming to New York. They'll let Donny's parents know.

When the ship bulging with anxious servicemen pulled into San Diego harbor, there was a rush to get to the side that would first face the dock. A loud announcement went out to "Hold your positions. Do not rush the dock!" That would be the last order George would ever get. At this moment, he was looking for a big Chrysler car and a girl in a blue dress. He had wired a special request. Unfortunately, he couldn't get a telegram back. But he was sure that she got the message.

Daisy was so excited as they rushed down the freeway to the port that she worried about staining her dress under her arms. It was another warm southern California day. The hope and anxiety that filled her heart made it seem like a hundred degrees. The traffic was now backing up as masses of people began to greet ship after ship coming in.

"Is that her over there?" George shouted.

The roar was beginning to build up as the gangplank went down, and the shore crews escorted the first troops down. George panicked. *Where is she? How am I going to find her in this sea of people? How would she even know to show up on this particular dock?*

Daisy spotted George and yanked her hand from her mother's grip. Lurching through the disjointed crowd, she flew into the arms of Corporal George Mitchell.

George grabbed her around the waist, "Daisy! How did you find me? You've got to be the bravest girl in the world!"

"George, you're limping. Are you hurt? Oh, I have a million questions for you. Both our parents are over by the fence. Let's go this way. I'm making you a big roast tonight."

A wide grin spread on George's face as other G.I.s embraced their loved ones.

After a long kiss, George stared into her eyes. "Daisy, remember what we talked about? You asked when real life would start. Well, now it can. What's playing at the movies tomorrow tonight?"

Discussion Questions

1. What was significant about the date on the newspaper's front page?

2. What was "island hopping"?

3. Why did Donny refer to Admiral Nimitz and his vacation home?

4. What is the meaning of the title?

The Protester

Washington Anti-War Protest

Amy Foster had just finished half a piece of her mother's apple pie when she realized that eating it all would just make those new jeans stretch to the point of popping. At least, that was how she visualized it. She thought if she could somehow associate disaster with eating too much, she might win the battle of the waistline. Not that she was plump, but she never wanted to get into that grey area.

Amy liked being thin. And she enjoyed being a normal girl in normal suburban New Jersey. She was a parent's dream. And in 1968, having a well-behaved child was not that predictable. There was a lot of rebellion across the land. The Fosters went to church every Sunday and thanked the Lord that Amy grew up with a love of family and was happy with her path to the future.

"Thanks, Mom. Great dinner," she said and started to clear the plates from the table, including her brother Brad's. She moved to the sink and started running the water to wash them.

"Sue Brady got her ears pierced today," Brad sang out from nowhere. He tossed that to the family as if it were a live hand grenade in the middle of the dining room table. "I saw her coming off the train from New York when I was walking home from school. Mandy and Pat were with her, and they couldn't wait to show me and Mike. Yuck! How can girls do that?"

A glass slipped out of Amy's hand and clanked on the counter. He was 16 going on 12, Amy thought. How can a boy be so stupid? She was going to Rutgers and knew some freshman boys who were as immature as Brad, but not many. She was a freshman too, but so far advanced from this Neanderthal posing as her brother. What sinister consequences could arise from putting a tiny hole through your ear? She was waiting for a response from her parents on this one. But Mr. Foster had turned on the TV, and the news occupied him as it did every night at 7 o'clock. And just as it did almost every night, the program led off with the same story: the Vietnam War. Amy walked in and sat next to her father. She wanted to feel the soft comfort of the sofa and her father's warmth. She needed to feel the calm center of the family, where all conflict dissolved. She felt safe from the world's complexity and danger. The story of the ears being pierced seemed to trail off as the sound of Walter Cronkite's voice reporting from a position in a forest of strange palm trees. His voice was interrupted by machine gun fire in the distance, just behind him on the large screen.

Cronkite was dressed in the usual flak jacket and hard helmet as he addressed the imminent arrival of another 10,000 more troops. "General Westmoreland today asked for even more support for a tenuous effort here in the Highlands of Vietnam. Local tribesmen, as well as the U.S 1st Infantry Division, are trying to turn back Viet Cong insurgents, but as we can see, the results are not very encouraging." The camera swept to the right, where all of America could see three men standing around a soldier lying still on the ground. One raised a bottle of fluids with a tube running from it into the arm of the dying man.

Mother sat down between her husband and Amy. "Oh my God, Sam. When are they just going to let this country alone.? Every night it's the same thing. Bobby Howard just left for basic training yesterday. When is it going to stop?" She was rarely emotional, Amy thought, but they all had heard of the draft claiming boys closer and closer to home. Neighbors were on the way to Southeast Asia, a place they didn't know existed a year ago.

"We've just got to hang in there long enough to show the world we mean business. We have to establish a strong enough government that can stand on its own two feet and then get the troops back home. But until then, we gotta give those commies three times what they're shootin' at us." Amy heard this line from Dad every time the war came up. It was his standard response, and she was beginning to doubt this strategy, even though she didn't know the answer.

The students at Rutgers certainly knew more than she did. They carried out "teach-ins" where students rallied to hear well-spoken rabble-rousers rap this country for issues like being too militaristic, greedy for power, and racist. Crowds outside the Student Union were getting larger, and the rhetoric was getting more anti-American. As Amy got up to do her schoolwork, she wondered if these protestors were getting too carried away with their speeches.

She understood the anger of the students, but somehow the passion escaped her. Of course, war was horrible, but people dying for a cause is noble. Isn't it? Does the American government deserve the venom she heard, like "imperialists, colonizers, and murderers?"

The whole conflict was ugly. To Amy, the more angry the speaker at the campus rallies, the more radically dressed they were. The boys had longer hair. The girls had holes in their jean and wanted to be called women. Sometimes it looked as if they dressed sloppily on purpose. What were they all trying to prove? Wasn't their disheveled appearance harming the image that would win people over to their side of the argument?

She could never join that side of the debate. How would her mother take her wearing her hair carelessly straight down? What would her father say if she wore a torn jean jacket, or worse yet, old army clothes or combat boots!? Amy remembered what she saw when she was downtown last week: a line of girls waiting outside the army-navy store, and she recalled an old line of contempt from her childhood days, "Ahhh, yer mother wears combat boots!". Here they were, buying them! She would never. Even if boys were dying for a reason she couldn't figure out, she would not join that crowd.

In January in New Jersey, very few outside events were scheduled, but these were busy nights, especially on college campuses. Rallies, speeches, and demonstrations were popping up all over the country. Dynamic speakers with loyal bands of student followers recruited new activists. As the military draft sucked up thousands of boys, who were nearly men. The the anti-war movement crept across college campuses, doing the same.

Dad said the protestors were a disgrace to the image of the university. Rutgers has always been a center for the highest academic achievement. Now it was little more than a platform for long-haired rabble-rousers. "Freedom of speech was one thing," he told her, "but when they cause damage as they did at Columbia or Berkeley and break the law, that's where I draw the line."

The next day she saw posters for another rally on campus to stop the army from recruiting there. She was more interested in seeing the winter fashion parade around the Ledge, the student center, and the cafeteria. Bell-bottom trousers, army field coats, bomber jackets ruled the day, and lambchop sideburns and goatees adorned male faces. English rock dominated the jukebox. The Who was playing at the Fillmore in New York that night.

When Amy came home from school, Mr. Foster asked almost immediately, "You don't have any classes on the campus tonight, do you, dear?"

"No, Dad. Amy sensed something was being left unsaid. Why do you ask?"

"Oh, no reason. Just nice to have you home every night," he replied, leaving for his den. In the time it took to dial a number on the telephone, she heard his lowered voice from behind the door. "If you need any help, Sergeant, I'll call Buck and James…. OK, OK…. Just offering. But we live in this town too, and I don't want to see any property damage, even if it **is** on campus."

Amy moved aimlessly about in the kitchen as her father came out of the room with an occupied look. She was trying to connect Dad's phone call with anything else happening, but she felt it was not her place to barge into his business.

Dinner was quieter than usual except for Brad's recap of basketball practice. The ham and potatoes were devoured in silence. And then, as the clean-up began, her brother began to relate how "far out" his friend Bill's new 8-track tape deck was in his old Chevy Impala. "We were riding around listening to Hendrix," he crowed, "Blew out one of the speakers."

Dad slammed his coffee cup down. "I don't want you listening to that crap, Brad Foster. And if you don't get a haircut with that two dollars I gave you by tomorrow, we'll have to go 'round and 'round. And don't think I can't still take you, young man!" The vein on Dad's forehead bulged, and his face turned red. He stammered to say more but stopped short of blowing his top as he gripped the table tightly. He consciously was making an effort to keep calm.

Amy's mother was taken aback at her husband's reaction. "It's only music, Sam."

"It's not just music. It's insurrection!" Her father got up and stormed into the TV room.

Amy followed and sat down next to her father. She understood that things were changing before his eyes that he wouldn't have any control over. A father needed control over his own family. Maybe he saw Brad slipping away. The war and the nation's reaction were tearing some families apart. The young pitted themselves against the old. Those old enough to die in this war were questioning those old enough to send them there. And they were asking more questions than just "Why?"

Amy casually glanced at the television as the President discussed something with a group of generals. Her father focused intently on the small black-and-white screen. Then the scene changed. A young reporter in camouflage battle dress stood to the left of a bombed-out building. His lips had been moving, and now Amy suddenly realized what he was saying.

"This morning, there was a large Buddhist temple here. Now it is a pile of bricks. In the boldest move yet by the Viet Cong, the city of Hue was attacked this morning in the middle of what was supposed to be a Vietnamese holiday truce. Thousands of North Vietnamese regular army troops stormed into the under-protected Holy City and demolished everything. Men of the 22nd South Vietnamese Division and the 82nd Airborne put up a brave resistance. Just over here, you can see the results."

The camera panned to the right, where a group of men slowly lifted black plastic bags onto a large canvas-topped truck. The reporter called them "body bags," and a chill went up Amy's spine. These bags were filled with dead men! Dead American boys. These bodies were the sickening evidence of this horrible war in this horrible place. She clutched her knees hard.

She gasped, and her eyes flooded with tears. It felt as if a bowling ball had been thrown into her chest. Her father turned to her and said, "Why don't you go upstairs, darling? Go do some homework. This is not something you should see."

Brad stood behind the sofa and chimed in, "Dad, you think that'll be over by the time I'm 18? I've only got a year and one month to go." Amy turned around and saw the eager look in her brother's eye. He was so desperate to please Father that he would go anywhere for him. She felt a rush of helplessness about to swamp her heart. She jumped out of her seat and ran up the stairs.

How could these people be shooting bullets into each other and bombing villages where women and children lived, and setting fire to life-giving crops? And how could they ...? There was so much tragedy in that faraway country. Even if the war were closer to home, what could she do? Would her brother Brad really want to go there?

She stood outside her bedroom and thought for a split second, then made a quick about-face and quietly, like a cat, dashed into Brad's closet. She emerged from the thick aroma of the boy's room with a pair of hiking boots in her hand. Like a burglar stealing jewels, she placed them in her room on the bed. Then Amy dashed lightly into her parents' bedroom shaking but determined. A strange new feeling of knowing what she had to do came over her. She had never defied her parents before, so she had to sneak around inside her own house. She slipped into the dark, stand-up closet and groped in the back for something. There it was—Dad's old navy pea coat. She remembered the thick, full-length winter coat from her father showing it off to Brad when the boy asked for some military souvenirs.

Of course, it was slightly bigger than a perfect fit. Luckily, the coat had shrunk some. And when Amy crept back into her bedroom, she found that her younger brother's boots fit her just fine with help from two pairs of socks.

She looked into her mirror with only the lights from the hall allowing her to see the reflection. She wiped the mascara from her eyes with a small towel and did the same to her lips. When she looked up again, she saw the face of somebody angry. There was no other way to feel. Tears would not get anyone anywhere now.

If she learned anything from her father, it was not to wait for others to come up with the solutions to her problems. Not that she had done much problem-solving in life. But this was different. For the first time, *she* wanted to be the one finding the solution.

She looked at the angry face once more. Without trying to make any sound, she descended the back stairs that led to the kitchen, eased the door shut, and marched out into the chilly New Jersey air. It was a good night to walk the five blocks fast. The rally was about to begin. College Avenue was packed with people. The police cars had stopped on both ends of the one block, officially shutting off any automobile traffic. No vehicle could push the waves of young gatherers anyway. The crowd was tense, so any car approaching would be greeted with resistance.

Amy wondered if that would mean police cars would be attacked. She felt a nervous excitement. From the looks on the faces of many protesters, anything could happen this night. She moved up to where the figures started to solidify. Some people had big cardboard signs with crude black lettering:

"U.S. Get Out of Southeast Asia Now!" "Hell No, We Won't Go!" They were chanting slogans when someone with a megaphone would start them up.

Amy was more concerned with rough-looking, radical types who looked like the more dangerous element on the streets. They had long, unkempt hair, and their clothes looked like they had just climbed down from a mountain refuge. The problem was that their signs looked heavier than the others since they were attached to baseball bats and two-by-fours. This wasn't just "peace and love" anymore. A word rang in her ear that she had never heard. *Militants!*

Oh, what was she doing here, she thought. And then she saw the TV cameras. Reporters for Channel 7 and Channel 9 were standing not too far away. Periodically portable lights sprayed parts of the crowd. When the light landed on certain sections of the protesters, they would turn and throw their fists up to salute the night's spirit. "My God," she wondered if her father would see her on the news tomorrow night! Just then, the camera crew's lights turned toward her section, and the radicals enthusiastically jumped and chanted, "LBJ, LBJ, how many kids did you kill today!" Amy raised the collar on her coat and turned away from the camera about 10 yards away. She moved on to get a better view of the speakers.

Over the heads of the thousands in front of her, she could see at least a dozen students on the steps of a small building with the letters 'R.O.T.C.' illuminated behind them. WABC was televising all the speeches. Whoever was up there intended to incite the crowd to action. There was a rumbling through the swarms of people around her as she began to be engulfed by new arrivals. Suddenly Amy realized she was now in the middle of a mob that was going to take over this building in protest of the war. They were going in!

"And we should not let this sinful signing of recruits take place on this campus," yelled one speaker through the microphone. "We cannot face the world and have them know that the officers, the leaders of this criminal act of aggression, joined this colonizing army right here at Rutgers! We have to take this building out of the hands of the war machine. Who will join me?"

At that moment, Amy felt a surge of bodies, and a volcano of cheers erupted from one end of College Avenue to where the police cars parked. Placards danced in the night air, and students' fists raised like punctuation marks in an electric rock-symphony. The student body became a high tide surrounding the two-story wooden house.

Suddenly a group of students bashed in a door right in front of her. The sound quickly alerted the police who moved forward. As the people around her surged toward, she could see a smiling sea of determined faces. Some students carried sleeping bags. *Were they going to sleep inside the building? Were they seizing University property?*

Hundreds of young people turned to face the police, now walking stiffly forward with nightsticks held chest high. They would feast on provocation and needed only a nod or a wink to start banging heads. She looked at one of these policemen who that afternoon was probably directing traffic over on George St. Now he was in riot gear with a helmet, flak jacket, and carrying a three-foot baton that could reach a student's head a split second faster than a small nightstick. And right over his shoulder, looking as if he would follow the line of police, was a familiar figure. It was her father!

His face was contorted into a mask of hate. He was right behind the blue line, seemingly ready to jump over someone to attack. "This is an illegal assembly! If you do not disperse, you will be arrested. Please leave the area now." A bullhorn broadcast the order over the taunting students. They were standing their ground in the face of the advancing police.

Amy froze. Her gaze locked onto that face she knew so well. He had not seen her yet. She had to move quickly. A few protesters cursed as they were pushed to the ground near her. Instinctively, she turned toward the building and moved straight ahead.

People were running now, and over the top of the crowd to the left, she could see mounted police atop huge brown horses with a look of fear in their own eyes. Her heart was racing. The police were advancing from both sides, and to the left was her father, who would melt her with one look. She lurched toward the ROTC building and somehow found herself on the porch. A door opened, and someone yelled, "In here!" She was safe.

Amy didn't come home that night. It was the first night she had ever stayed away from home without her parent's permission. Lines had been drawn between many conflicting sides that night, and one was between father and daughter. After that night, there would be many more nights where she would tell herself she should stay away for good. She had her ear pierced the next day before returning home.

"That WAS you I saw out there, right Amy? You've joined the mob?" He saw her again on the evening news the next night. He pointed to the television. "My own daughter!" He moved down to the end of the couch, giving her an icy stare.

"Remember that car I was going to get you? Forget it."

Brad joined the U.S. Army the day after high school graduation, and the Fosters became another American family stuck to the TV for the six o'clock news. The generation gap became a great gorge in 1968.

Discussion Questions

1. How did age differences affect where people stood on the Vietnam war?

2. Why was the ROTC building the site of the demonstration?

3. For what kind of issues would you be willing to demonstrate?

Coming Home

I Pledge Allegiance

"Leon, you see who's coming down the street? It's your brother, Nazzy. Did you know he was coming back today? Look at that big bag he's carrying."

Two Cuban men lurched out of their seats, and the dominoes game on a steaming hot street in Miami, 2003. A muscled-up young Latino man in olive-green army fatigues slowly walked up to the sidewalk table game.

"Leon!" the visitor cried.

"Nascimento, you pendejo, what are you doing here. Come over and get wit me."

With the joy beaming from the soldier's face, he places a backpack on the ground and hugs his brother.

"Leon, you didn't get no better lookin' did you?"

Leon was a proud possessor of a huge, curly Afro and wore a baggy tee shirt. "Naz, I didn't want to take all the ladies from you when you got back, so…I'm still the same. You look like you been in that gym down on South Beach. And where'd you get that tattoo?"

"Bro, you can't be in a tank division in Kuwait without a tattoo. It's supposed to be a picture of Mommy with a cross, but the guy had a shaky hand. Not easy to get good ink in Baghdad. What are you up to these days? How come I didn't get a letter?"

Leon stares at his brother's combat uniform, trying to change the subject. "Where's Bagdat? What's the three stripes for?"

"I'm a sergeant in the U.S. Army, bro." Naz, short for Nascimento, puffed out his chest.

Leon offered his brother a plastic camping chair, and the three men sat down.

"Man, you know I don't write. My English speaking is terrible, even worse when I write it. I heard you were coming back, so I got you this cigar." He took a crushed brown hunk of tobacco from his baggy jeans and handed it to his brother. Leon turns to his friend Santos, a tall thin boy with a smirking smile planted on his face, who hunches his shoulders. "Well, I was carrying this around for a couple of days."

Naz chuckles, "Better be Cuban, at least. Where you working now, bro? You look like you need some carnitas and red beans. You skinnier than Santos over here. You ok?" Naz nodded at Leon's friend.

The three sat down and kicked back as Naz rested both hands behind his head. He put the ragged chunk of tobacco on the table. No cigar.

Leon says, "I been good. Worried about you. Hard to take care of Pops makin' two bills a week fixin' tires around that stupid place. I ain't got a raise since you left."

"You're still at Jose's?"

"Yeah, but I'm workin' on my GED. Gonna' get a real job. Takes a little time."

Naz looked a little skeptical. "Where is that GED school? You got a book? Show me."

Leon looked hurt. "We…we…keep our books there. You know, so they won't get stolen."

"Yeah, sure. Santos, you believe him, right?"

Santos winces, pushing both hands straight up and out, "Don't get me involved in this."

"Tell you what, men. Let me buy myself a Welcome Home drink down at Hector's, and you're both invited. I'll tell you a couple of stories about tanks in the desert."

Leon rose like a jack-in-the-box and said, "Please do, and tell us what the heck a Kuwait is."

Operation Desert Storm called American troops up in the all-volunteer army to challenge a dictator in the Middle East. A threat of mass destruction weapons, possibly nuclear, provoked a collection of U.S. partners to travel across the globe in a war that only lasted a few weeks. Hundreds of tanks and other armored troop carriers crossed the desert of Iraq and its neighbor Kuwait in a flash. In the sky, the most highly developed aircraft filled the skies and bombed the city of Baghdad. French, British, and Italian soldiers also participated in downing the forces of Saddam Hussein. They showed the world how allies in the West could work together.

Inside Hector's, a busy Cuban restaurant just down the street, Naz, Leon, and Santos debated the mini-war. In the noisy room, the men had to lean toward each other to be heard.

"But Naz, we only got to Miami a couple of years ago, and you're riskin' your butt for this new country? Mama would have smacked you and told you to stay home."

"Well, she never made it from the Island to see what we see here, did she? Dios la bendita (bless her). That stinkin' doctor in Havana couldn't take care of her, and now she's dead. We go to the clinic here every time we cough and get pills to take home. She wudda' loved to join us. And how do you like your dinner, Leon? It's on me because I just reenlisted too. We get a bonus. How do you like that?" Naz stood back and smiled at his little brother.

Santos peered over his fried pork steak at the restaurant and asked, "How much you get"?

"Plenty, but the biggest payoff is getting my citizenship papers. Anybody who served who wasn't an American yet can get the papers in a couple of weeks. Do the ceremony and boom, you're in."

"Wow, you ain't gonna be Cuban anymore?" Leon's eyebrows squeezed lower with a skeptical look.

"Oh, I'll be Cuban, but Cuban-American, best of both worlds," Naz crowed.

Santos offered some skepticism, "Now you gotta' pay taxes. Go to jury duty."

Naz grinned, "Maybe get drafted someday."

Leon looked sad. He wanted to be in the U.S. for his own well-being, but turning into something he was not didn't feel right. Would he have to write in English? Wear a collared shirt all day, and buy a big car? What would it feel like to be American?

As weeks passed, life around Calle Ocho, Miami's 8th Street in English, dragged on with Santos and Leon wearing greasy and oily coveralls, in the heat of the South Florida summer. Their uniforms of the day from the tire store didn't show any medals like his big brother got. Naz, on a 30-day pass before his next assignment, attended English and Math classes at the local high school most evenings to get a GED. Not that he needed it at the Naturalization Ceremony the next week, but the more papers, the better he thought. Most military vets who served overseas automatically were awarded citizenship upon return to the States, but Nascimento wanted to be naturally adopted.

Leon was not convinced his big brother should become a U.S. citizen. He saw the papers Naz had left on the kitchen table. Somewhere it read that each American had to defend the country "against all enemies foreign and domestic." What if even new Americans had to fight Cuba? No way. And you had to speak good English and know who the third president of the United States is, and, man, it sounded like too much stuff. Best to just let it be, but I hope Naz doesn't think I'm just un chicharo (a lazy guy). Maybe someday.

Naz awoke one day in their simple house on the western side of the city, made some strong Cuban coffee, and put on his only white shirt for his trip to the Claude Pepper Federal Building. The bus on 8th St. went directly to the old grey building that reached up into the sky. Too many of his aseras (buddies) had gone there to pay off fines, late taxes, or other immigration violations. Today, however, he would take a stand. He would be an American. The bus ride was unusually smooth this day, just like Nascimento's thoughts on remembering the pledge. He didn't want to look dumb. Other people would say it simultaneously so he could speak it with them. He had passed his interview and a ten-question history test, so all that was left was to take the pledge, and he would be a naturalized citizen of the United States. The Cuban-born veteran of Desert Storm scrambled down the stairs of the bus a little hesitantly. He stood up straight and entered the biggest building he had ever been in. This soldier was coming home.

So many different kinds of people! Naz noticed the room full of foreign-born adults, many dressed in their native garb. One lady had a scarf on her head, and another older man wore what looked like a uniform, but he was wearing a skirt underneath it. What the heck? He remembered a guy back in the 101st Airborne showed him a picture of his father at a party with a kilt and a big pearl-handled knife sticking out of oversized socks. And he remembered hearing the sounds of a bagpipe somewhere in a parade in Miami on Memorial Day. He must have been a Scotsman. Not so strange after all, he figured. And with a "Tap, tap" from the podium in front of the 20 or so new Americans, a tall Anglo man in a tan suit began to welcome them.

After the man's speech, it was time for what Naz dreaded most, the Naturalization Oath. The girl at the office in the local post office said he'd have to memorize almost a whole page. Then she chuckled. But he practiced in front of the mirror dozens of times. Leon kept telling him where he went wrong as he stood with a copy. Little brother butted in, "that I will bear arms on behalf of the United States when required by the law. Naz, you sure about this?"

Naz turned from the mirror and whispered, "L'il bro, I'm already bearing arms on behalf, remember? I just reenlisted last month. And I used the bonus to buy you're GED books. Remember that too."

Now he was nervously ready, hoping the Asian-looking kid next to him would help with a loud voice to follow. But oh, lucky day, a big print page appeared on the white wall next to the American and Florida state flags. The Naturalization Oath of Allegiance to the United States of America. Whew! He could read it.

With one big voice, the pledge began. "I hereby declare, on oath, that I absolutely and entirely renounce all allegiance to any foreign prince, potentate, state of sovereignty, of whom or which I have heretofore been a subject or citizen; that I will support and defend the Constitution and laws of…."

They repeated the oath together. Because Naz knew the words so well, his head swiveled over to his left, where he spied that big head of hair sticking straight out of the small crowd of onlookers, like a brown Jimi Hendrix. Brother Leon! What was he doing here? Leon was gripping a stack of white papers in his hand.

"And that I take this obligation freely," the man at the podium continued, "without any mental reservation or purpose of evasion; so help me, God." BOOM! The room burst into a joyous, jumping mass. Naz did his mini-meringue dance as he slid over to his little brother.

"Leon, I remembered the whole pledge!" he said, lowering his voice and smiling quizzically, "What are you doing here?"

Leon offered his hand. "Congrats, bro, but I saw that big screen up there too." He laughed out loud as the other new citizens began shaking hands with each other. Naz turned around and shook the hand of the man from Scotland, then the lady with the scarf on her head. Finally, he turned to Leon, "So what are the papers?"

"Well, I figured if all you tough Americans are gonna bear arms against all enemies, foreign and domestic. I better get on the right side of that. These are the application papers for citizenship, brother". Leon's face beamed up to Naz. "I'm proud of you."

"And I'm proud of you, L'il Leon. But you know it may take much longer than I did. I already serve in the military." Naz put his hand on Leon's shoulder.

"I know. It might even take longer than my GED, but I'll do it even though all the wars are over. I don't feel like I'm cut out for jumping out of airplanes or slitherin' around in a smelly ole' tank, but I wanna' join. And then, I wanna' own that tire store."

Nascimento looked serious for a second. "Bro, no one knows if the wars are over. No one knows."

"Well, if the time comes, and as it says in the Pledge, when required by law, I would be ready. I would say, I do."

"Hah!" Naz howled at Leo, laughing at his brother's new pledge. "Leon, I do? Hah, that's a whole different ceremony, and don't rush into that other one either." Leon cracked up with his brother, and they walked with arms around each other's shoulders out into the warm Miami streets. One man a citizen, the other becoming one.

Discussion Questions

1. What kind of job did Nascimento have in Kuwait?

2. What did Leon's brother do between assignments?

3. Why doesn't Leon write in English?

4. Write a paragraph describing how you would feel about joining an army in a country you just moved to? What kind of mixed feelings might you have?

Answers to the Questions in Part One

<u>Judgement At Sea</u>

1. How did Billy keep track of time?
    B. He carved notches in his boots

2. The best meaning for the word "Placid" is?
    C. Peaceful

3. Why was the name Courageous an appropriate name?
    A. The pilgrims were courageous.

4. What was a minor problem on the ship?
    D. Seasickness

5. Where were the lemons, limes, and oranges from?
    B. Italy, Spain, and Portugal

6. Why did people get Scurvy?
    C. Not eating the right foods

<u>Witch Hunt</u>

1. What was Parris' occupation?
    C. a Pastor

2. Where was Salem?
    C. Massachusetts Bay colony

3. Who led the group of girls?
   B. Mary and Elizabeth

4. What was the punishment for being a witch?
   D.Either A. B. or C.

5. What did Mary pretend to see in the church?
   C. a yellow bird

6. In a paragraph, what did the villagers learn from this episode?

Surprise at Ft. Ticonderoga

1. What is the best description of where the Fort is?
   D. On the New York/Vermont border

2. Why were Emily and her mother patient about their position in life?
   C. They wanted Father to get his promotion.

3. When does this story take place?
   A. Before the Revolutionary War.

 4. How does the reader know that Ethan Allen is a worthy enemy of the British?
   C. His writing has been in the newspaper.

5. What word best describes the takeover of the Fort
   C. imagined

Into The Heat

1. Why did Mrs. Miller "turn the tables" on Uncle Robert?
    A. She was being inhospitable.

2. How does the reader know that Uncle Robert is not anti-British?
    A. He says, "His Majesty."

3. Benji's father:
    A. felt protective and responsible for the safety of his brother.

4. To who did Mr. Miller sell his wood products?
    A. Anyone who had his price.

5. Why was Mr. Miller so quick to respond to his brother's advice?
    B. He was afraid that his brother might turn Benji in for spying.

Fisherman Two

1. What was the biggest reason for the War of 1812?
    C. It was a conflict for dominance over the seas.

2. What is surprising about the kind of bombs they used?
    A. They burst in the air.

3. Why did Gordie have a "painful grin"?
    C. He was proud and afraid at the same time.

4. Why did Gordie's father wonder if the flag would be there the next day?

    B. He didn't know if the Americans would win.

While Waiting Wharfside

1. How does the reader know that at least one of the explorers is a military man?

    C. He is named Lieutenant Clark.

2. What is meant by a "civil meal"?

    A. One that is not made up entirely of corn.

3. What was Thompson doing away for two and a half years?

    D. He was exploring and mapping the country.

4. How did Thompson describe the men on the docks?

    C. bird-like

5. What would be the next thing, besides a good meal, that one of the men would want?

    D. A bed

The Book of Life

1. Why did Bobby bring books home for Toby?

    B. Toby couldn't go to school because he was black.

2. What's the best meaning of conspicuous?

    C. To be easily seen

3. How would you describe Toby?
    A. Mature

4. What is shrapnel?
    B. Parts of an exploded bomb.

5. Why was Bobby's mother most concerned about the boys'
reading?
    A. She didn't want to be accused of helping slaves to
read.

6. Since Maryland wasn't a Confederate state, it is all the
more surprising that Toby would be _____ to the South.
    B. Loyal

Honor to the Brave !

SEA FENCIBLES,

And only for Twelve Months.

Where an honorable situation now offers to all young men, whose hearts are inspired with love for their country.   There is no situation which offers more advantages at this eventful crisis, than the SEA FENCIBLES, and that in defence of the Ports and Harbors of the U-nited States, only.   Come *then my*

Brave Patriots,

embrace this opportunity of tendering your ser-vices to your beloved country.   Repair imme-diately to my *Standard* Water st. No. 21, near Cumberland Row, or to the Barracks, Liberty *street, Old Town,* where you have an oppor-tunity of crowning yourselves with the laurels of your country, and receive *Twelve Dollars* in advance, and *Twelve Dollars* per month in addition to Navy Rations.

JOHN GILL, Capt. U. S. S. F.

feb 11   d1m

CAVALRY!

WANTED GOOD HORSEMEN IMMEDIATELY

FOR COMPANY

12TH NEW YORK CAVALRY

3d IRA HARRIS GUARD.

— NOW IN THE FIELD, AT NEWBERN, N. C. —

BOUNTIES.

FOR NEW RECRUITS		FOR VETERANS	
STATE BOUNTY	$75	STATE BOUNTY	$150
GOVERNMENT BOUNTY	100	GOVERNMENT BOUNTY	400
ADVANCE PAY	13	ADVANCE PAY	13
PREMIUM	2	PREMIUM	2
	$190		**$565**

This Company will leave in a few days to join the Regiment, which is now in the department of Maryland

JAS. W. SAVAGE, Col. Com'd'g.

Co.

Union Army Soldier

WAAC
DAN V SMITH
THIS IS MY WAR TOO!
WOMEN'S ARMY AUXILIARY CORPS
UNITED · STATES · ARMY

I WANT YOU
FOR U.S. ARMY
NEAREST RECRUITING STATION